The Power of
Positive Prophecy

Other books by Laurie Beth Jones

Jesus in Blue Jeans: A Practical Guide to Everyday Spirituality

Jesus, CEO: Using Ancient Wisdom for Visionary Leadership

The Path: Creating Your Mission Statement for Work and for Life

Grow Something Besides Old: Seeds for a Joyful Life

The Power of Positive Prophecy

Finding the Hidden Potential

in Everyday Life

Laurie Beth Jones

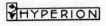

New York

Library of Congress Cataloging-in-Publication Data
Jones, Laurie Beth.
The power of positive prophecy : finding the hidden potential in
everyday life / Laurie Beth Jones.
p.   cm.
ISBN 0-7868-6350-1
1. Prophecy—Christianity. 2. Christian life. I. Title.
BR115.P8J65   1999
133.3—dc21   99-20548
                                                          CIP

Book design by Chris Welch

First Edition

10   9   8   7   6   5   4   3   2   1

*To Dee Jones, my friend, confidante, and
prophet who always sees—and speaks—
a positive future for me and everyone she
meets. She truly lives her mission, which is to
"inspire, administer, and embody greatness."
How blessed I am to have her as a co-worker
and friend.*

Contents

Section II
Sources of Prophecy

Section III
How to Prophesy

Introduction

As I was doing research for my book *The Path: Creating Your Mission Statement for Work and for Life*, it struck me that the people who had a sense of mission about their life also had a sense of destiny—a destiny which oftentimes had been prophesied to them by others. As I reread the Gospels with this question of prophecy as my filter, it became keenly evident to me that many of the actions of Jesus were based on what had been prophesied to him. "I must do this to fulfill the prophecy," he said time and time again.

Biblical scholars have observed that prophecy takes up 40 percent of the Old and New Testaments. My research has led me to believe that at least 40 percent of our own lives are based on prophecies which we have either been given, or claimed for ourselves. Consciously or unconsciously we are being pulled into the future by the magnet of prophecy. What we believe about the future so often does come true—for individuals, for communities, for the world. The intention of this book is to help each of us accept the responsibility of speaking words which teach, encourage, and challenge one another to a higher level of seeing and being. Prophecy is not only knowing the mind of God—it is also about knowing *your* mind—how it works—what it believes—what it is consciously and subconsciously pulling you toward.

As I began to immerse myself in the subject of prophecy, I discovered that prophets are everywhere among us—determining with their words the futures of clients, companies, children, patients and students. Prophets come in many forms—one to suit all of us. Stockbrokers study the intestines and entrails of companies, prophesying which will live, which will fail, much as the prophets of old did. A physician walks into an examination room with a patient's chart in front of her, and the trembling patient asks, "What does this chart mean, doctor? How long do I have?" And then the physician begins to prophesy.

The Psychic Hotline is the number one best-selling infomercial of all time. For three dollars a minute you can have a trained telemarketer help predict your future. Not content with that? Just flip through your local newspaper then, and find your horoscope. An upscale hotel in Kansas City has a designated telephone line for daily horoscopes. The instructions read: For Daily Weather Report, punch one. For Daily Horoscope, punch two. Not long ago at my local YMCA I noticed that they have the daily horoscope taped to the counter of the snack bar. Eat a muffin while determining your future.

Why is prophecy so important to human beings? It has been said that we are the only species on earth that can exist in the present while simultaneously worrying about the future.

Webster's Dictionary defines prophecy as: (1) The foretelling or prediction of what is to come; (2) something that is declared by a prophet, especially a divinely inspired prediction, instruction, or exhortation; (3) any prediction or forecast; (4) the action, function, or faculty of a prophet.

After much research and reflection, I have expanded that definition to be: *Prophecy is any word or action that influences an outcome.*

Words and actions are the true tools of prophets, and they are available to us all. While some people choose to focus on events which are prophesied, I choose to focus on prophecies that shape people, because ultimately, it is people who shape events.

And while some people devote much time and effort to discerning the meanings of the words of Nostradamus and the book of Revelations, drawing elaborate time lines and depicting graphic illustrations of multiheaded beasts, I believe that the spirit of Christ would have us more concerned with the runny nose and disheartened frown of the child in front of us, or the struggling student who is on the verge of quitting school.

The true spirit of prophecy is not about predicting cataclysmic events. Even Jesus said no one knows when the end will come, and for every heavenly sign and wonder that someone correctly interprets, thousands more pass by without being noticed. The true spirit of prophecy is encouraging the people around us to see themselves as God sees them—in light and love and power.

Prophecy with a "c" is a noun. Prophesy with an "s" is a verb. The word needs both forms because nothing is set in stone. God prophesied destruction to the city of Nineveh through the prophet Jonah, yet the destruction did not happen. Was Jonah a false prophet? No. He predicted an outcome for the city if they did not change their ways—but they did change their ways. Therefore, the destruction of Nineveh, although predicted, was not an immutable event. The people still had a major choice in the outcome because of what, and who, they chose to believe.

This principle is vital: we have a choice in the directions of our lives, and our beliefs and actions determine our outcomes.

In my seminars when I began to ask people to try to remember someone who gave them a positive prophecy that affected them greatly, their answers were revealing.

One man said, "I grew up in an alcoholic household where I never heard a positive word. On my way home from school I would always stop in at Jimmy's, the local dry cleaner, because he kept candy on the counter. He got to know me, and told me one afternoon, 'Michael, you are a very smart boy. Someday you are going to run a very big business.' I would listen to him in disbelief and return home only to get called a 'dog' and knocked around by my dad. But you know," he said with tears forming in his eyes, "Jimmy the dry cleaner was the only person I can remember believing in me." He paused a moment to catch his breath and gather the reflection that was forming inside him. "Today I run a multimillion-dollar health care organization, just like Jimmy predicted. I guess you could say that a dry cleaner was the prophet in my life."

Another woman shared, "I came from an unhappy home as well. On weekends I would go into town and ride the elevators in the big fancy hotels just to get out of the house. They had elevator operators back then, and this particular woman took a liking to me and let me ride up and down with her for hours. One time we stopped at the fourteenth floor and she looked at me and said 'Rose, put your head out and look at all these fancy offices here.' I did, and then she said with a smile, 'Someday you are going to have your offices here, on this very floor.' " Rose revealed that she eventually went on to become a lawyer. She now is a senior partner in a law firm which has offices on the fourteenth floor—just as the elevator operator predicted. An elevator operator was the prophet in Rose's life.

The key determinant in these two stories is that a prophet was sent with a positive message to each of these children, and the children chose to receive and believe it—even though the prophets did not fit the stereotypical image of an old man in a robe.

The Power of Positive Prophecy is designed to raise your mind to a new level of awareness about the messages God is sending to you and through you every day. Perhaps you will never rise to the level of a Daniel or an Isaiah. Perhaps you will never accurately predict a single major event in time. But if your words can help clear the path or remove a stumbling block for even one person in God's kingdom, you shall receive a prophet's reward.

To think that only a select few are called to be prophets, and to think that prophecy is merely the accurate foretelling of events, is to miss the larger picture. If Jesus had wanted us to focus exclusively on studying the end times, he would have spent his days on earth explaining in detail the visions of the prophet Daniel or interpreting the dreams and visions of Ezekiel.

Instead, he devoted his time to teaching the qualities of kindness and compassion. He taught his disciples how to discern the inner as well as the outer needs of the people gathered before them. He talked about a Samaritan who helped an enemy who had fallen into a ditch. He spoke words of encouragement to a vertically challenged man who had climbed up in a tree. He reached out his hand and lifted up a woman who moments before had been destined to hear only the sound of stones ending her life. He told the fearful and ambitious to consider the grace of the lilies when their fears started to growl. He looked at everyone around him and said, "If you have seen me, you have seen God.

And I am here to tell you that God loves you very much indeed, and has good things planned for you—if you will only receive and believe."

This is the spirit of prophecy that I hope permeates this book.

The work is divided into three sections. Section one details "Types of Prophecy," intended to help you recognize the various subtle forms prophecy can take. While the Prophecy of Declaration might be one which is obvious to everybody, I hope, like a good tour guide, to help you also recognize the prophecies which might lie hidden in the weeds of Defeat, or be shouting at you in Play, like a laughing child dangling from the monkey bars in the playground. The final chapter in this section, entitled Negative Prophecies, also contains thoughts on How to Overcome Negative Prophecies, since they are so prevalent in today's society.

Section two details sources of prophecy, and is intended to help you learn to recognize the messengers of God, who may be disguised as a kindergarten teacher, writing words on a chalkboard, or a brother sending you a check in the mail so you can continue with your art classes. Parents are prophets. Friends are prophets. Aunts and uncles and grandparents and bosses and co-workers are prophets—all shaping futures with their words. I have included a brief chapter on angels and animals, which have historically been used as God's messengers as well.

Section three offers thoughts on how to become a prophet. Once you become aware of the many forms that prophecy can take, and how a few choice words might hold the key to somebody's destiny, how could you not want to be a prophet and share that gift with others? Since I believe prophecy is a gift that can be cultivated, I offer steps so that those who either have or seek the gift can become better at it. Included in this section is a chapter entitled "Words of Caution," as prophecy can be used for evil or for good.

I close with just one example of "A Prophecy Unfulfilled"—to emphasize the vital need for prophecy in our communities. A few pages are allotted for you to write down prophecies which have been given to you, followed by a prophetic pledge which you are asked to take and sign in front of a witness.

Moses looked out across a band of hungry and weary people murmuring discontentedly in the desert. He lifted up his face to heaven and sighed "I wish that all of the Lord's people could prophesy." *(Numbers 11:29)*

My prayer is that you, too, will seek the gift of prophecy, and I dedicate this book to help make that happen.

Section I

Types of Prophecy

Learning to Recognize the Forms Prophecy May Take

The Prophecy of Declaration

The Prophecy of Names

The Prophecy of Defeat

The Prophecy of Desire

The Prophecy of Expectation

The Prophecy of Culture

The Prophecy of Protest

The Prophecy of Play

Self-fulfilling Prophecies

Negative Prophecies

The Prophecy of Declaration

"He spoke, and it was created."
Psalm 33:9

*S*ome time ago I was visiting friends in Albuquerque. Yvonne and I were sharing our morning tea when in stumbled Antonio, a usually gregarious and affectionate eight-year-old. He sullenly sat down at the table, pulled his cereal bowl close and began to eat. "Antonio," asked Yvonne, "can't you give Laurie a breakfast greeting?" "No," he said. "Why not?" she asked, beginning to get upset. He raised his head, looked at her with exasperation and cried, "I can't, Mom, because it's not morning in my throat yet."

How we laughed and laughed. I think, however, that Antonio's words are descriptive of many of us. We can't seem to give each other pleasant greetings because we feel "it's not morning in our throats yet."

This is a tragedy, because all of creation stems from the spoken word. "God said, Light be, and Light was." *(Genesis 1:3)*

Words are the building blocks of civilization. With words we enchant, entice, enthrall, entertain, and educate. (And that's just the *e*'s!)

Jesus said we would be judged by our words, so they needed to be measured and weighed out carefully.

"But I say to you that for every idle word men may speak, they will give account of it in the day of judgement. For by your

4

words you will be justified, and by your words you will be condemned." —*Matthew 12:36*

Yet we carelessly toss and jangle, unleash and release floods of words, many of them curses or complaints. Are we aware of what we're doing? I think not.

In J. Rodale's *Synonym Finder*, we find that "word" means term, name, expression, ideogram, symbol, sign. "Word" also stands for assurance, promise, pledge, warrant, guarantee, oath, vow. "Word" means news, tidings, report, notice, information, intelligence, command, directive, prescription, ordainment, rule, edict, mandate, charge, bidding. The phrase "word for word" means exact, precise, accurate, close, faithful, honest, strict, undeviating, explicit, express, unambiguous, unequivocal.

"He's as good as his word," is a compliment we don't hear often enough these days. People who realize that "word" means bond or pledge or command use words more carefully.

As I was writing this book I had an amusing incident occur which was perhaps sent to remind me of the importance of this chapter on words. I was at my home in Texas, talking with Dee Jones, my administrator, on the phone about the future direction of our company. I told her that I wanted us to be like a beehive—with lots of bees going out, dancing around the flowers gathering pollen, and then returning to the hive to help make honey. Dee said that was a very powerful image, and we talked about a few other items and then hung up the phone. I left to run some errands, and when I returned I noticed that a few bees had gathered around a lampshade in the living room. "How odd," I thought to myself as I carefully trapped them in jars and then set them free. When I awoke the next morning I heard a buzzing sound in the living room. "The yard man must have come early," I thought to myself as I groggily made my way toward the kitchen. I was not prepared for what awaited me. There, in the living room, were thousands of bees. They were swarming on the windows, the sofa, the coffee table, the fireplace. I hurriedly made my way through and called the exterminators, who said they couldn't come out until the following day. I then called Mom, who said, "Honey, make sure they aren't killer bees." "How does one know?" I asked. "Wait a minute—I'll look it up," she said as she retrieved one of her hundreds of reference books. "It says here that the only way to tell the difference between killer bees and regular bees is that killer bees have an extra membrane in their wings. Do you see any extra membranes?" she asked. "Extra as opposed to how many?" I asked. "This difference is usually only detectable under a microscope . . ." she continued to read. There was a long pause. Then she said quietly, "Honey, run!" "Don't call me honey," I yelped as I made my way to a friend's house to await the pest control man. He came the next day and shook his head. "I've never seen anything quite like this," he said. "They must have thought the queen had moved in here. Looks like they came down through the fireplace." "Very funny, Lord," I thought to myself as I awaited the time when I could make my safe return.

You may think this story is an exaggerated example of the power of words to attract and create. I don't think so. That's why I don't let anyone curse around me. I truly believe that words are among the most powerful tools of the universe. Jesus thought so, too.

We are all constantly prophesying the future by the very words we speak. Is the future we are prophesying a positive one—or a negative one?

One of the root prefixes for "prophet" is "pro"—which is derived from Greek and Latin, with the meanings forward, advancement, movement. The second root of the word prophet comes from the Greek "phetes"—which means speaker. So the word "prophet" gives us the picture of a speaker who goes in front of someone in order to advance their movement.

One of the most important aspects of prophecy is that it must be spoken. Prophecy must be *heard* in order to be received. A renowned musical trainer was consulted by opera singers who, for some reason, could not hit particular notes within an octave, even though the notes fell well within their range. After conducting extensive tests on their vocal cords, the trainer decided to check their hearing. He discovered that the singers could not *express* notes they could not *hear*.

The same is true for us. I expect that many, if not most, of the men and women who have found themselves in prison today cannot express positive lives because they never heard the sound of one.

We are only now beginning to learn the power of sound to create, motivate, and destroy. Today militaries are spending millions of dollars to create weapons which emit high frequency blasts, blasts which are capable of destroying entire armies. As strange as that might sound, it has historical precedent. When the priests followed the instructions of God and blew on rams' horns while they circled the walls of Jericho, the walls came tumbling down. Some experts and archeologists claim to have found scientific evidence that the walls crumbled as the result of some mysterious vibration.

In the book of John we are told, "The Word became flesh and dwelt among us." *(John 1:14)*

I am convinced that the people we see walking around every-day are also "words become flesh." The question is whose words? Yours or mine? God's, their parents', or someone else's? Whose words are we fleshing out with our deeds and actions? And what will be the consequence of those words?

In some ways, prophecy is like a blue pan. Let me explain what I mean by that. When I first moved into my new home in Texas I drove past a neighbor's backyard and noticed a plastic white goose standing on the back porch. Chuckling to myself that at least it wasn't a plastic pink flamingo, I continued on my way. One day, however, I noticed that the neighbor had put out a small blue plastic pan of water for the goose to stand in. "This is getting ridiculous," I thought, and I drove up to the fence to take a closer look. Suddenly the plastic goose burst into hissing, flapping, charging life—and came running at me with full force. I beat a hasty retreat, marveling at how big that plastic goose really was.

Whenever I rode by after that, however, I couldn't help but notice that no matter where my neighbor placed that pan, the goose would always be sitting in it. It didn't seem to occur to the goose that there was a whole yard for it to explore. The small blue plastic pan was home. I began to wonder why my neighbor didn't get a larger pan for the goose, since it spent all its time there. For that matter, why not dig out a whole pond for it? Or even a swimming pool? There was no shortage of space in the yard. "Poor goose," I began to think as I drove by. "Confined to a small blue plastic pan in such a huge backyard."

Now I know that all prophecy is like that small blue pan of

water, and we are like that big white goose. Human nature will always gravitate to a place it feels is "home," no matter how small or limiting that place might be. As prophets pour out their words, they are setting up blue plastic pans for us—sometimes big, often too small.

"You'll never amount to anything. You're going to end up in jail just like your father." There the goose will stand. "You're going to be a great leader some day. You will make your home among the mighty." And there, too, the goose will be, flapping its wings and swimming around the pool in comfort, feeling that this space is indeed home.

Prophecy pours out a form for us to fill.

And words are the tools of prophecy.

Careless words or overarching generalizations can become prophecies that haunt us. One woman said in a seminar recently that her parents had told her, "You can do anything you set your mind to." This woman said she has spent her life going from one endeavor to another, flailing about seeking the career that was right for her. When I began to ask people in my seminars what some negative prophecies were that they had received from their families, a surprising number said that being told "you can do anything" had actually put a great deal of pressure on them, delivering a shroud of anxiety rather than a mantle of comfort. I am reminded of the *Peanuts* cartoon where Charlie Brown is walking around with his head down. When Schroeder asks him what the matter is, Charlie Brown sighs. "There is no greater burden than having 'potential.' "

Well-meaning generalizations are not enough to qualify as a true prophecy, if they set the person adrift in a sea of possibilities with no compass and no support.

Not to speak is to shout. Not to prophesy is to prophesy. One of the more touching stories I have heard in my seminars is that of a man who has suffered most of his life with uncertainty. When I asked him if he remembered his parents telling him anything positive he said when he was a little boy his bedroom was located right next to the kitchen. After he had gone to bed he would sometimes hear his parents speaking about something his teacher or coach had said about him. "I remember pressing my ear up against the wall trying to discern exactly what was being said. I never could quite make it out though. The walls were too thick and my parents whispered. So I never knew if what had been said about me was good, or bad. That question seems to haunt me still." Perhaps his parents came from the school of thought that taught you shouldn't praise children because they might get a big head. How tragic that this man never heard a word of praise from those closest to him.

In the Path Training seminars I often ask people to write down what their parents' unfulfilled dreams were. Usually at least half of the group cannot articulate a dream that their mothers or fathers had which was even spoken or talked about. Not surprisingly, these people have the most challenging time when it comes to writing down their own dreams or visions for the future. By their parents not sharing with children their personal dreams, the subconscious message they are sending is "Dreams don't matter." Not to speak is to shout.

Words spoken casually as generalizations can become broadcasts, as well. One seminar participant shared with us that her mother used to go around muttering, "We're not from the best stock, you know." This woman grew up in Appalachia, and went on to get married, have kids, and work as a teacher's aide. When

I asked her why she never went on to become a teacher she replied, "Hearing that we were not from the best stock made me afraid that no matter what I accomplished in life, someone would discover our family background and expose me. So, I have always kept a low profile and tried not to be noticed."

We live according to the words which have been declared for us, either consciously or subconsciously. Words are the prophecies which pull us, guide us, shape us into who we are to become.

The words we declare—for ourselves and for others—are prophecies.

Questions:

1. Which tool is the most vital one for any prophet, and why?

_____

_____

2. Describe your personal "blue pan." What size and shape is it? What words make up its water?

_____

_____

3. Why is not speaking really speaking volumes?

_____

_____

4. Why must words be chosen and spoken so carefully, especially around children?

_____

_____

Meditation

Dear Lord,
The world we live in was created through your spoken word. Help
me to realize that you have given me, too, words which can create
worlds for the people around me—either barren, empty landscapes
or gardens full of nurturing fruit and flowing streams. As King
David once prayed to you, I also pray. Truly, O Lord, may the
words of my mouth be acceptable in your sight.

Amen

The Prophecy of Names

"Better a good name than costly oil."
Ecclesiastes 7:1

$\mathcal{N}$aming things was the first task and privilege given to human beings in the Garden of Eden. "So from the soil Yahweh God fashioned all the wild animals and all the birds of heaven. These he brought to the man to see what he would call them; each one was to bear the name the man would give it." *(Genesis 2:19)*

Throughout the Old and New Testaments, names are taken very seriously. "You shall not misuse the name of Yahweh your God, for he will not leave unpunished anyone who misuses his name." *(Exodus 20:7)* Quite often, human names were changed to reflect a change in personality or status. Abram had his name changed to Abraham after he believed God, and left the land he knew, to travel to an unknown place. "No longer shall your name be called Abram, but your name shall be Abraham; for I have made you a father of many nations." *(Genesis 17:5 King James Version)*

One man received his new name in a dream. "God said to him, 'Your name is Jacob, but from now on you will be called not Jacob but Israel.' " *(Genesis 35:10)* Zacharias was a priest in the days of Herod. He and his wife, Elizabeth, were barren. However, one day the angel Gabriel appeared to him and said, "Do not be afraid, Zacharias, for your prayer is heard; and your wife Elizabeth will bear you a son, and you shall call his name John."

Zacharias replied, "How shall I know this? For I am an old man, and my wife is well advanced in years." And the angel answered him, "I am Gabriel who stands in the presence of God, and [who] was sent to speak to you and bring you these glad tidings. But behold, you will be mute and not able to speak until the day these things take place, because you did not believe my words which will be fulfilled in their own time." Sure enough, the little baby boy arrives. "So it was, on the eighth day, that they came to circumcise the child; and they would have called him by the name of his father, Zacharias. His mother answered and said, "No; he shall be called John." But they said to her, "There is no one among your relatives who is called by this name." So they made signs to his father—what he would have him called. And he asked for a writing tablet, and wrote, saying "His name is John." So they all marveled. Immediately his mouth was opened and his tongue loosed, and he spoke, praising God." *(Luke 1:13-19, 59-64)* For some reason the angel was insistent that this child be called John. (Evidently, the forces of heaven didn't think "Zacharias the Baptist" had the proper ring to it.)

Shakespeare opined, "What's in a name? A rose by any other name would smell as sweet." Apparently, that's not so with bananas. A worker at a grocery store was instructed to put some darkened bananas on sale at half price, or 49 cents a pound. Although the peels were blackened, the insides were still good, and the store manager wanted to move them. The enterprising worker had another idea. He put up a sign that read "Argentine Bananas—$1.19 a pound." The bananas sold out in one hour. What we call something does affect perception.

Few events are as prophetic as the naming of a child. One philosopher said "What you name, you control." And certainly the names we give to our children convey our hopes and wishes and fears and dreams for them. Their names often become their prophecy.

The naming of children is a responsibility parents must take seriously. In the book *Beyond Jennifer and Jason*, the author, Linda Rosenkrantz, offers numerous studies which show that names have power.

In one university study, six equally attractive young women (as determined by student polling of photographs) were arbitrarily assigned names like Susan, Bertha, April, Harriet, Amy, and Ethel. The photos matched with names like Susan, April, and Amy outscored the names of Bertha, Harriet, and Ethel by as high as 60 percent. When the names were switched yet again on the photos, Susan (formerly Bertha) got a higher score.

In another study, freshman English compositions were arbitrarily assigned author names like Robert, Wilhelm, Bill, Edgar. The compositions whose author had the more common names of Robert and Bill received higher scores, sometimes as much as 30 percent higher than those with unusual names.

A prison study revealed that inmates whose names were Lethal, Odour, and Menace had a higher recidivism, or return to prison rate, than those with more common names. The explanation was that children with names like that were automatically set up to fight to defend their name.

Names alone are not the sole determiners of future. However, names do set up expectations of behavior and response.

One special education teacher who attended our Path training seminar stated that they used to have classes for Down's Syndrome children called "Remedial Training." The new school

principal switched the name of the class to "Leadership Devel-
opment Training" and the children's scores, and their eagerness
to attend the class, rose significantly.

Dee Jones, my administrator, recently chose her own title.
Technically, she is the Chief Operating Officer, making sure all
systems are firing on all cylinders. She told me one day that she
didn't like that title for herself because it sounded like her task
was full of operations and repairs. The title she now has chosen
for herself is Manager of the Flow of Opportunities, which is, in
fact, what she does. She looks at every task in front of her as an
opportunity to serve, and is diligent about directing how they
flow in toward us and out from us toward others. A subtle shifting
in words has caused all of us, including her, to see her talents in
a new light.

Sometimes the names we give others can become a heavy burden for them.

One day we got a letter from a reader who was sharing that
he felt overwhelmed with his life responsibilities, and wasn't sure
he was up to handling them. I happened to glance down to the
bottom of the letter where he listed his name. His name was
Robert Johnson IV, as in Fourth. This man grew up carrying three
generations on his shoulders. No wonder he felt overwhelmed.

A friend of mine shared that he had struggled all his life with
a feeling of being second best because of his name. He was named
William, like his grandfather. It wasn't carrying his grandfather's
name that had been the problem, but the fact that a little boy
had been born to his parents before him, named William. The
first little William died after only four days, and was buried in
the family plot. "When we would go to the cemetery and visit

his gravesite, and I would see my name there in the stone, I felt like it should have been me—that maybe my parents wished he was alive, and I wasn't."

Names can also bring a child a sense of comfort and joy. The singer/composer/conductor Bobby McFerrin shared in a delightful interview on "60 Minutes" that he clearly remembers the day he learned what his name meant. "Robert—blessed by God," he said slowly with a smile. "And McFerrin means 'man of iron.' So here I was, eight years old, already being told that I was going to be a man of iron, blessed by God. I remember thinking to myself 'I'll never be afraid again.' And I haven't!" he laughed. A person who knows the meaning of his or her name carries a prophecy that can serve them well.

Reginia Clark learned the meaning of her name from a stranger. Placed in a Home for Children by parents who were unable to care for her, Reginia felt abandoned and unwanted. One day as she was walking along the sidewalk the headmaster of the school stopped and looked at her. "Reginia—that is such a pretty name." Reginia was embarrassed that such an important looking man was paying attention to her, yet she was thrilled at the same time. "Do you know what your name means?" he asked her. "No," she said softly. "Reginia means 'queen.' And that is exactly who you are, and that is who you will become," he said with a smile, looking directly into her eyes. That moment was a turning point for the lonely child. Eventually, Reginia went on to a successful career and a happy marriage. She and her husband established a charitable remainder trust for the home where so much kindness had been shown her. "This is where I learned what God had in mind for me. I felt like an abandoned orphan, but Mr. Robert Hayes showed me that I was a queen."

I was having lunch with a young mother-to-be, who was helping me with this manuscript. We were discussing the subject of
names, and she said she was going to name her daughter Sarah
Nicole, which means "Princess" and "Friend of the people." She
said that her grandmother had called and begged to have the little
girl named after her. "My husband and I gulped when we heard
that," Heather said. "My grandmother's name is Adeline." Fortunately, her grandmother relented and allowed them to name
the baby after her middle name—Sarah.

If you ever want to see my friend Catherine flare, just call her
Cathy. She will give you a look that amounts to a nuclear melt-
down. Raised by an elegant woman and a cattle rancher, Catherine has created a career for herself that has allowed her to drive
a red Jaguar, wear a Rolex watch, and build a house that is a
combination sanctuary/showplace. Everything she has is the finest and the best. When one of my friends asked me in awe "What
is it about her that makes her always seek—and receive—the
finest of everything?" "Well," I said, "consider the legacy of her
name. 'Catherine the Great.' She grew up believing herself to be
a queen, and that is how she expects to be treated." "Wow, just
my luck to be named Polly," laughed my friend. "No wonder I
only get cracker crumbs." In the heartwrenching eulogy delivered by her brother the Earl of Kent, Princess Diana was remembered for her name. "How ironic," said her brother, "that Diana
was named after the goddess of the hunt, and she became the
most hunted woman of our time."

I have two love birds named Chirico and Celine. Celine fell
ill not too long ago, and lost most of her feathers and part of her
left claw before the antibiotics kicked in and saved her. She has
not sung since the disease took its toll, despite Chirico's constant

care and affection. Yesterday I brought home Celine Dion's CD with "The Theme from *Titanic*" on it, and began playing it while I worked. Suddenly I heard *two* birds singing in the sun room. I rushed downstairs, and there was my little love bird Celine, sitting on a perch and singing her heart out. "Oh, you like your namesake's voice, is that it?" I asked as she bobbed her head up and down and poured out her own version of "The heart will go on and on." What's in a name? Maybe more than we think. We all want to sing out the sound of our names.

I am sitting in Grigg's restaurant writing this chapter on my portable computer. I come here because I love the atmosphere and the sounds of people all around me. They set me up with my own little table by the fireplace in the corner, and bring me nonstop tea while I write. The woman who is the hostess here is named Mrs. Kitchen.

In San Diego there is a family-owned funeral home that has been in the family for generations. It is called The Goodbody Mortuary Company.

Scanning through the phone book last week looking for the phone number to Thrifty's drugstore I came across the listing "R. K. Thyfault, attorney at law."

Ann Landers recently carried a story about a woman who fell off a bar stool and was fatally injured. Her family is now suing the establishment where she was drinking, The city where this lawsuit was taking place? Sioux Falls.

My friend's dentist's name is Dr. Flossy. I know of an osteopathic physician in Maine called Dr. Kneebone. An article in the *Wall Street Journal* by Eleena "De Lisser" lists the names of Daniel Harp, the music teacher; Susan Spicer, the chef; Chris Roach, a pest control operator, and John Hamberger, a restaurant consultant. The man intent on creating the first human clone is named Richard Seed.

A recent headline told the tale of a schoolhouse shooting that had been interrupted when a young student stepped in front of the gunman and calmly told him, "Put the gun down." When asked about his courage, the teen hero said, "Courage? I believe this is what I was sent here to do." His name? Ben Strong.

The great race horse Man of War lost only one race out of the twenty in his career. The name of the only horse ever to defeat him was "Upset."

On Main Street there is a restaurant that has failed repeatedly, despite the constant changes in management. It is called The Fowl Place. Investors are still trying to figure out why no one wants to go there.

USA Today recently carried an article about angry airline passengers whose travel plans had been interrupted. One couple said that they were furious about getting bumped from two different airlines. Their names were Mr. and Mrs. Bumpus.

The automobile Chevy Nova bombed in Mexico, even after the company paid a fortune to have a proper name selected. The experts failed to translate the name into the various languages of the foreign markets they would be entering. In Spanish "no va" means "doesn't go." I had to chuckle when a Mexican friend predicted that the Mazda Miata wouldn't fare too well in Spanish speaking countries, either. When I asked why, she said, "Because in Spanish 'miada' means 'wet diaper.' "

Fortunately, not being given a melodious or common name is not a curse that cannot be overcome. Having an unusual name hasn't hurt Oprah Winfrey. Neither has it hurt the career of Whoopi Goldberg.

A friend of mine had adopted a black Lab/dalmatian mix from Animal Rescue who she held great hopes for being a wonderful, intelligent, loving companion. She named him Bowser. Unfortunately, he turned out to be a fence jumping escape artist who coud leap five-foot fences in a single bound, wriggle out of collars, and climb trees. He always greeted her, and her guests on his two hind legs, hopping up and down. His antics were driving her to distraction. She was about to give him away when her little eight-year-old-neighbor came over and began playing with him.

Susan was pruning her rosebushes, wondering what to do with "Bowser the headache" when she overheard little Rebecca cooing to him, "Hello, Circus Dog." She turned to her and said in awe, "Do you know that he can walk across the backyard on his hind legs? Yesterday I threw a frisbee that got stuck in the tree and he climbed up the steps to the tree house and got it!" Rebecca's renaming Bowser "Circus Dog" changed his fate. It gave his frustrated owner a whole new perspective on him. Now she's having him professionally trained, and the trainer has commented that this is one of the smartest dogs he has ever seen.

Names are powerful tools which identify, shape, or control others.

Mary Virginia Micka wrote in her book *Greeting: All Rounds Returning*

> Say
> who I am
> Set
> our two fires climbing.

Our names are meant to say who we are. Let us choose and guard them carefully.

Questions:

1. What does your name mean?

_____

_____

2. What does the name of your spouse or significant other mean?

_____

_____

3. Does your name suit you?

_____

_____

4. Would you be willing to change it if it didn't?

_____

_____

5. What is the importance of "naming" people and things?

_____

_____

Meditation

Dear Lord,
Names have proven to be of great importance to you. Help me be
aware of the significance of the names I choose or apply to others,
including myself. Give me the courage to change a name that
doesn't suit me, and give me a deep awareness of how names
actually shape what people become.
*   Amen.*

The Prophecy of Defeat

There is a saying, "Whom the gods would destroy, they crown with early success." In a society that worships success, this is a hard saying. People who teach that God wants us to be rich overlook the fact that many times God needs us to be poor. "Blessed are the poor in spirit, for theirs is the kingdom of heaven."*(Matthew 5:3)* It is through the trials that our good fortune comes.

A man named Jim was born the eldest and the only son. His mother worked at home and his father was a physician. Descended from Jewish immigrants, Jim was taught early on the importance of hard work. "Yet somehow I picked up from my dad that there were only two really successful people in the world," Jim said. "One of them was a brain surgeon in New York, and the other was a world class violinist. Since I neither wanted to be a brain surgeon nor a violinist, I understood that I would therefore never really measure up to my father's expectations."

Based on some encouragement from his mother, Jim took up law, and began a thriving law practice in Southern California. His career meant nothing to his father, however, who would constantly talk about the riches of music or medicine. This only widened the gap between them, and soon Jim and his father were barely speaking. His father's health soon deteriorated to the point where he was given only two months to live. Being the eldest son, it was Jim's responsibility to go spend time with his dad. "Even in his weakened condition Dad was brittle and unyielding. He alienated the nurses, the doctors, the caretakers, and ignored everyone's care and advice. Finally, in desperation I said, "Okay, Dad, it's your choice to die alone. I'm going home.""

Jim returned home to learn that his long-time family friend had embezzled his entire life savings, along with those of two hundred and fifty other investors. Jim, who had always been blessed with excellent health, suddenly began losing weight. "Everything I had built up financially and healthwise for the future was suddenly blown away," Jim said. "I stood looking at this barren wasteland in my life, and knew that there was only one place to turn. I had to return in humiliation and defeat to my father." He flew back to his father's side, and slowly, sadly admitted that he had lost all his earnings through a swindle he had been too busy to catch. "I knew that my father was going to blast me for my stupidity, so I just put my head down and prepared to take it."

Instead, his father reached out his hand, put it on Jim's, and said, "Just tell me how much you need." Jim told him the amount, and his father wrote him a check without a word. Jim looked at the check, and said, "Dad, aren't you even going to yell at me? This is a lot of money." "No, son," his dad said. "We all make mistakes. And what is a father's money for if not to help his children." There was an instant change in his father's demeanor towards Jim and his two sisters. He began to call them every day just to see how they were doing. He began to say he was going to outlive the doctor's predictions. Jim's health began to return, also. Three months after their reconciliation, Jim's father died suddenly in his sleep.

Jim shared this story with tears in his eyes. "Everything had been healed between us. I realized, at last, that he loved me. He said he was proud of me and my success with my family. And then he died." Jim is convinced that it was only his total financial defeat that brought him and his father back together again. And through this defeat came a healing that revealed that death for either of them was not an issue anymore. Their relationship became alive.

Author G. K. Chesterton says, "In everything that yields gracefully, there must be resistance. Bows are beautiful when they bend only because they seek to remain rigid. Rigidity that slightly yields is all the beauty of the earth. Everything seeks to grow straight, and happily nothing succeeds in so growing. Try to grow straight and life will bend you."

A wine connoisseur I know named Dominic once told me that the grapes which are the best are those which grow in sandy soil. "Because the grapevines have to dig deeper into the sand to find their nourishment," he said, "the wine becomes even richer."

My friend Catherine says that most trees are shrubs that just keep getting pruned. I was astounded at this. And yet as we walked through the rows of plants and trees for sale at the nursery, she would bend over and say, "See? All these little knots on this pear tree have been cut away. Somebody always has to keep pruning them or they'll have no shape at all, and bear very little fruit."

The prophecy of defeat could almost be called the prophecy of pruning—and plowing.

I love living in the farmlands of the fertile Rio Grande Valley. To reward myself for a long day's work I often take a drive up an old farm road. The corrugated rows of dirt, interspersed with silver rows of water, have a hypnotic effect on me as I sail by in my white pickup truck, listening to music. Sometimes a field that not long before had been flat and empty is covered with rustling rows of corn. Sometime in the early spring the farmers plow and slice and turn the earth into chunks of dirt that are so large you can barely lift one of them with both your hands. When I see the land being turned upside down, I know that planting time is near. What seems like defeat for hardpacked, solid ground is actually positive prophecy.

I was enthralled to watch the PBS special "Liberty: The American Revolution." In my mind I had somehow formed the opinion that we Americans just whipped the British in a few decisive battles, and that was that. My chronology would have gone something like this. "We got really mad about the tax thing, dumped a bunch of tea into Boston Harbor, Paul Revere went racing through the streets at night waving a lantern telling the soldiers that the British were coming, everybody got up, got dressed, and as soon as George Washington crossed that really cold river in Trenton, we fired our muskets and the Redcoats surrendered." Kind of instant victory by microwave. Therefore I was fascinated to learn that George Washington lost every battle he waged except two; that the strategy of the American general in the South was to have his men "fire and run." He said, "I want the British to understand that there is no battle we are too proud to lose." The Americans would hightail it into the bushes like a bunch of scared rabbits, drawing the neat and tidy Redcoats further and further from their camp. Soon, they began running low on supplies, and had to take whatever they needed from the formerly sympathetic Americans who considered themselves loyal to the crown even after war had been declared. Eventually, the citizens began getting angry at the imposition of the British, and infuriated by the casualties of American soldiers. These series of defeats led them to unite as a nation in their resolve to rule their own destiny apart from the British crown. An early victory would have been a hollow one, it seems. It took time, and many defeats, to unite and shape the New American.

One British soldier recounted in his journal the final march to surrender their weapons. He said, "And who had defeated the greatest army in the world? Not a well-dressed, highly disciplined military force, but a group of farmers and printers and noblemen, wielding whatever weapons they had. When we looked up on the hillsides into the faces of our captors, who were standing looking down on us with pitchforks and muskets and shovels, it seemed we were looking at a new breed of men." Each defeat had been etched into their faces—and into the soul of a new nation. The early series of defeats had become America's positive prophecy.

If you go to the Sixteenth Street Baptist church in Birmingham, Alabama, you will see the place where a horrible act of violence served as a wake-up call for this country. One sunny Sunday morning, September 15, 1963, a bomb went off, killing four little girls attending Sunday School. "At that moment," said Walter Cronkite, "Americans understood the real nature of the hate that was preventing integration, particularly in the South, but also throughout America." The bomb that took the lives of four innocent children unwittingly ignited the civil rights movement, and shook the conscience of a nation. It is out of the rubble of this defeat that we as a nation began the march back to our soul.

People magazine recently shared the story of a man who found victory in defeat. Don J. Snyder reveled in his academic life. On his $36,000 salary he lived in a comfortable home, with a teaching schedule that left him plenty of time to write. Looking forward to tenure, Don was shocked when handed a pink slip. His life suddenly began to unravel. In his book *The Cliff Walk: A Memoir of a Job Lost and Life Found* Snyder tells how being forced to finally take a carpenter's job suddenly freed his mind to write the novel he had been promising to write all along. He found the physical work rewarding, too. "You're not waiting for somebody to call you into an office and tell you your work is good. You look at it and you know it's good." His book was purchased by Disney for movie rights, so money is no longer a worry. Yet Snyder still keeps his job with the construction crew part-time. "I've found a peace in working with my hands," he says. "A peace I can't part with now."

The artist was thrilled with his new commission. "We want you to paint a picture showing a cowboy herding cattle on our ranch," said the matriarch, shoving a Polaroid of a cattle-herding scene in front of him. Since this woman owned one of the largest ranches in the Southwest, Tom knew there would be a nice fee paid. He eagerly began his work, painting a cowboy on a prancing paint horse trying to redirect a voluminous herd. When the work was complete, he called her and told her to come see it. She said she'd be there Friday, but Friday came and went with no word or sign of the woman. He called again and she apologized, said she'd be by soon, and then hung up. Weeks and months went by, and Tom realized with a sinking feeling that his commission had evaporated. The painting was now his to do with what he wanted.

Looking at it with a mixture of sadness and "what the heck"

he thought that the paint horse looked like a rocking horse he once had as a little boy. So, just for the heck of it, he painted the faintest hint of rocking horse rails underneath the hooves of the paint horse.

Another customer happened by, and fell in love with the painting. "That reminds me of my son daydreaming about being a cowboy someday. Why don't you call it 'Daydreams'?"

And that is how "Daydreams" became one of the most sought-after prints in the world of cowboy art. The artist took a defeat, and turned it into a victory, by putting his own heart onto an unbought canvas.

Betty Ann Bird was unhappy with her work. She was doing an excellent job, all right, judging by her clients' satisfactory re-marks, and by her bank account. But she wanted to use her gifts in another way. Trained as both a nurse and as a business ad-ministrator, Betty Ann knew how to help hospitals avoid dupli-cation in various departments. In a world of nonstop mergers and acquisitions, she and her firm, Quest Leadership Consulting, were very much in demand. Nevertheless, she hated handing over reports which she knew were going to cause people to lose their jobs.

She went on a spiritual vision quest, of sorts, attending an International Conference on Business and Spirituality, and brain-storming with friends about finding a new Path for herself.

Finally, she decided that she was going to put on a Call to Values Conference for Health Care Executives, and give top leaders in the industry a chance to share their concerns and their dreams about the sensitive topic of maintaining values in a down-sizing, bottom line–oriented world. She and her business partner, Lisa Dahlberg, mailed out fliers, bought ads, got speakers, and then were dismayed when the three hundred anticipated attendees dwindled down to a mere thirty.

Discouraged, she called up the speakers and the few people who had registered and said that it was not going to happen. She was going to have to cancel the event.

"Oh no you're not!" declared one of the speakers. "I will come and speak for free. This is too important to let go." Other CEOs of major health care systems rallied around her—saying that this event had to happen, and urging her to reschedule it later in the year. Bill Pollard, CEO of ServiceMaster, a five billion dollar company, offered to fly in and also speak for free. Dough Hawthorne, president and CEO of Texas Health Resources, called and gave invaluable tips and leads, as well as offering to speak. Fred Roach of Baylor University, Dan Wilford of Memorial Hermann Healthcare Systems, Mary Lynch of Sisters of Charity Health Care Systems—all called to say, "This event needs to take place, and we will help you." So Betty Ann took a deep breath, rescheduled, and sent out another round of fliers and ads. The first Health Care Fellowship: A Call to Values conference took place three months later, with sixty-five attendees, and major industry news coverage. The response was so enthusiastic that the "alumni" are insisting on making it an annual event.

Betty Ann "lost money" on that conference, but what she did was invest in a new future and direction for her own company, as well as sounding a trumpet call for an industry in need. Her web site is now getting triple the inquiries, and she is on a first name basis with people who ordinarily she might not have been able ever to meet.

The "defeat" of nearly canceling the event caused others to realize they needed to help her, and ultimately caused it to be much more successful. Betty Ann shared her thoughts. "If everything had gone without a hitch, and I had not admitted my discouragement and vulnerability, I never would have formed the incredible bonds with these leaders that I have now."

Sixty-five people attended the first conference. Who knows how many will attend the second one, now that Betty Ann and Lisa took their "Quest" in another direction.

Some years ago, when my advertising agency and my real estate portfolio began to crumble around me, my friend Catherine and I went for a walk along the beach. I told her with very heavy sighs that it looked like I was going to fail at both my businesses, and I began to weep. She walked along silently for a few moments, and then said, "Laurie, this is the best thing that has ever happened to you. I see God's hand all over it." "What?!" I exclaimed. "God doesn't like failure!" "Oh," she laughed. "This isn't failure. This is just God clearing the way for a new beginning—one that's built on *your* dreams, and not your father's for you."

Her prophecy of encouragement kept me from plummeting into a pit of despair. I remember thinking once that I would rather die than fail. How wrong I was about mislabeling a series of events "failure." As John O'Donohue shares in his book *Anam Cara*, "It is the holes in the lace that render it beautiful."

Questions:

1. Which defeats have turned out to be prophecies, or signposts, to triumph for you?

_____

_____

2. Who is experiencing a sense of defeat right now that you might help reframe as a prophecy toward greater success?

_____

_____

3. Define "failure." What does it mean to you?

_____

_____

4. Take your current "defeat" and imagine a happy ending. Write it down.

_____

_____

Meditation

Dear Lord,

In you my weaknesses are made strong. I realize that your intent for me is always to grow, and never to fail or die. You delight in my ultimate triumphs, and yet you test me in order to make me stronger. Help me to see my present "defeats" as containing seeds of ultimate blessing and true joy, and help me to deliver a message of hope to others who might be thinking they are forever doomed to a life of "failure."

Amen.

The Prophecy of Desire

"May the Lord grant you the desires of
your heart."

Psalm 37:4

$\mathcal{A}$ woman in one of my seminars shared that while growing up, she learned the saying "It must be a sin if I want it so badly." Barring a desire that is illegal or immoral, I believe that God often speaks to us through our desires. Desire can be a positive motivating force that determines an outcome. Without desire, not much will happen, as I learned when I went to get some copies made.

The banner outside the store said "Get Your Copies Made Here." Delighted that this drugstore would save me a twenty minute drive, I walked in with my ten pieces of paper, and made my way to the big copy machine. I laid the first sheet down and realized quickly that there was no power to the machine. Looking up, I noticed a uniformed worker casually strolling by. "Excuse me—could you help me with this machine? It doesn't seem to be working." "Yeah," she said, "that's because it's not plugged in." I waited for her to plug it in but she just stood there, fooling with some receipts that were on the counter. "Well, could you plug it in?" I asked. "I don't know where the outlet is," she said without looking up. "I would imagine it's fairly close to the machine, or they wouldn't have placed it here," I added helpfully. "No," she said. "I think they brought the machine in last week, and in the meantime built this counter up around it, but I don't think I can reach the outlet under the counter." "Would you try?" I asked, trying not to get impatient. She said, "I already know I can't reach it." She stood there looking at me defiantly.

Since I am working on the areas of self-mastery, I had to consciously keep my body from crouching into a growl, pounce, and attack position. "Could you tell me where I might find the manager, then?" I asked. "Why?" she said sarcastically. "The manager's arm isn't any longer than mine." At this point I spun on my heels and walked away, finding a manager counting bars of soap several aisles away. I informed her of the problem, and she said, "I'll get right to it." Meanwhile, there were now three more people standing in line at the copy machine, so I went about gathering my other items and decided to return to the machine later. Within two minutes I heard the hum of the copy machine.

The woman who had refused to help me was now at the cash register. When I got up to her I casually nodded over to the copy machine and said, "I guess the manager's arm was longer after all."

I share this story because it is such a graphic illustration of the prophecy of desire. Without taking out a tape measure I suppose I couldn't be exactly sure, but my guess is that the manager's arm was just about the same size as the employee's arm. The difference was "Desire."

As I was walking through the park later that day, I held up my hand and thought, my hand is probably the same size as the hands of Emily Dickinson, Mary Cassatt, Florence Nightingale, or Mother Teresa. My hand is probably close to the size of Michelangelo's, or Georgia O'Keeffe's, or the firefighter that saved the elderly woman last week. My hand is probably the size of Albert Schweitzer's or Martina Hingis's or Oprah Winfrey's or Abraham Lincoln's. In fact, we all basically have hands and arms that are not much different in size. What makes the difference between what we do with them? "Desire."

And the truth is that most of us have so little of it that we end up leading lives of quiet desperation. The word "desire" has many connotations—everything from sexual desire to spiritual desire. In going through my *Strong's Bible Concordance* I was interested to note the many scriptures that have the word "desire" in them. In several Psalms, David asks that the Lord allow him "to see my desire upon my enemies." In one Proverb we are told that "desire accomplished is sweet to the soul" and in another we are told that the "desire of the slothful killeth him." *(Psalms 59:10, Proverbs 13:19, Proverbs 21:25)* Clearly, "desire" is a loaded word.

The desire I speak of here is the same desire Jesus spoke of when he said, "Whatsoever things ye desire when ye pray, believe that you have received them and you shall have them." *(Mark 11:24)* The desire I speak about is the divine longing we feel—the drive which will cause us to overcome incredible odds and bring something to pass which might not otherwise have happened.

I was astonished to read a story not too long ago about a young couple who were only a year into their marraige when the husband went out jogging one morning and was struck by a car. The injuries were so severe that the wife was told that he would not live. She insisted that they keep him on life support, and sat down with tears streaming down her face, caressing the same hand that just that morning had touched her cheek in a loving goodbye. Now it was hooked up to a roomful of machines, and her husband was going to die. Then this woman did the most amazing thing. She called up all her friends and asked them not only to pray, but to bring their Bibles to her at the hospital, which they did. After the Bibles had been delivered she asked the people to return home so she could be alone with her husband.

She opened up the Bibles to every passage she could think of which promised answers to prayer, and laid those Bibles at her husband's head, feet, and hands. Then, she stretched herself out on top of him and challenged God to answer her prayers and the prayers of the people, and said that she knew that God was capable of restoring her husband. She read aloud the passages about Jesus bringing back the little girl from the dead. She recalled the passage where Elijah had stretched himself out on a dead child and how the spirit of life had returned. And she lay there, praying for hours.

The nurses and doctors shook their head in sorrow as they walked by, leaving her alone in her grief. The next morning just as the sun was coming up her husband wiggled his hand. She jumped off him and began kissing his fingers. Then his eyes slowly opened and he lifted his head and said, "Darling, what are we doing here? Let's go home." That man did not die. He lived. How much did this woman's sheer faith and desire have to do with his recovery?

Desire is one of the most powerful magnets of the human spirit.

I heard a story recently about a boy who constantly asked his mother if they could have a dog. Being a single mom who was barely able to make ends meet, she told him that they couldn't afford one, but maybe someday they could. "Oh, that's all right, Mom," he said one day. "I know we're going to get one. I've already seen him in a dream. He's a bright red Irish setter and his name is Pat." She smiled at the boy's enthusiasm and felt a sinking feeling, knowing there were simply no funds to purchase a pet, much less a beautiful Irish setter.

Two weeks later an Irish setter followed the school bus home. Her son's eyes gleamed with delight as he said, "Can we keep him, Mom? Can we keep him?" "Son, I'm sure this dog belongs to someone. We have to run an ad in the paper so his owner can come claim him." She ran the ad in the lost and found, and sure enough two days later up drove a station wagon. The owner got out and thanked her for finding his dog. "I just can't keep him home," he said. "The sad part is I'm leaving town, and have no place to take him. You wouldn't want him, would you? He sure does seem to like your boy." She said that yes, they could certainly give him a happy home, and thanked the man profusely for such a beautiful animal. As he was driving off, he leaned his head out of the car and shouted, "By the way—his name is Pat."

A woman I know had been single for a very long time. She had given up on men, resigning herself to living alone. Yet one day she was in a card shop and on a whim picked up a gag gift called Boyfriend in a Box. This clever creation came from a woman who evidently had friends who were bemoaning the state of affairs of not having a boyfriend, so this woman created a series of boyfriends in boxes, which came complete with a five by seven photograph, a wallet-size photo, a statistic sheet on the man, a handwritten note saying, "I'm sorry," a signed card from a florist saying, "I love you," and a guarantee that this boyfriend would never forget your birthday or cheat on you. Anyway, Wanda picked out the boyfriend entitled "Doctor Dave." She took it to the office and kept it on her desk as a joke. Every day she would laughingly greet her boyfriend "Doctor Dave." One weekend she attended a self-improvement seminar. During the morning she noticed that this one man kept looking at her, so at the break she introduced herself and asked his name. He told her it was Michael and they began visiting. He then asked her out for lunch the following day. Wouldn't you know it—he was a doctor. She was struck by how much he even resembled the photo, with the exception of being a few years younger. When they were exchanging e-mail addresses, he listed his as something like mds@compuserve. com. When she asked him what the "d" stood for he said "My middle name is David." They are now involved in a very intense and promising relationship.

Now, did this woman having a visualization of her ideal boyfriend help create it? You tell me.

> Trust in the Lord, and do good:
> Dwell in the land, and feed on His faithfulness.
> Delight yourself also in the Lord,
> And He shall give you the desires of your heart.
> —*Psalm 37:3-4 King James Version*

Questions:

1. Regarding your desires, where are you acting like your arm is shorter than anyone elses?

_____

_____

2. What has kept you from reaching out for what you want?

_____

_____

3. If you were to have a confidential conversation with your most trusted friend or counselor, what would you list as your heart's desires?

_____

_____

4. Write them down here.

_____

_____

5. On a scale of one to ten, one being low, rate how strong your desire is in each area.

_____

_____

6. Describe the difference between wish and desire.

_____

_____

7. Turn up the volume of your prayers. Do you believe that God knows what you really desire?

_____

_____

Meditation

Dear Lord,

*I say, like King David did in Psalm 38:9, "Lord, all my desire is
before thee." Help me to clear away the clogged arteries and
distractions and half truths which are preventing me from receiving
your goodness and your joy. Purify my heart to want and seek
only you, and what you would have for me, and then give me the
courage to want that with all my heart and soul and mind and
strength. Let my arm be longer today than it was yesterday.*

Amen.

The Prophecy of Expectation

There is a difference between expectation and desire, even if it is a subtle one. While desire implies a secret longing, expectation implies an outfront positive certainty. Expectation carves a path for the universe to come to your door. In so doing, it becomes prophetic, helping to create the future. For example, if your dog sits and looks up at you expectantly while you are eating, you will more than likely give him food. His look of expectation proves to be prophetic. Expectation does not act surprised when something good happens, because that was the anticipated outcome.

Children are masters of this technique. Hearing I was going shopping for a horse, Antonio, my eight-year-old friend, sent me this handwritten letter on a piece of school notebook paper.

Dear Laurie—
Oh how I love you!
What are we going to name my pony?
Antonio

It was accompanied by a crayon drawing of a tall person (me), a little person (him), and a pony with a big toothy smile on its face.

The fact that I did not yet have any ponies didn't phase him.

Guess who went looking for ponies, rather than quarter horses the next day.

One of my favorite verses in the Jerusalem Bible is from the book of Wisdom, chapter 8. It reads "Wisdom makes choice of the works God is to do." I have pondered this verse for many years. The idea that wisdom, or a personality of reason, actually directs a waiting God to act, is an amazing example of cooperation and co-creation.

Jesus said if you ask with anticipation and expectation, never doubting in your heart, you will receive what you asked for. *(Matthew 21:21)*

Perhaps the greatest example of expectation in the Old Testament is the story of Noah. When he heard a prophetic word that a flood was coming, he didn't doubt it. He went straight to Home Depot and started buying up all the lumber he could find. He did not say, "Well, if this should happen, God will somehow manage to save me and my family." He believed the prophecy and started hammering in total anticipation of the rain starting as planned. When the flood came, he floated safely away, while those who weren't expecting a flood drowned.

As I'm writing this, I am sitting in my living room at the ranch. The sun is streaming in through my twenty-feet-high windows, while the shadows from the trees outside make a dappled, dancing pattern on the floor. If I turn my head to the left I look out on my white Arabian stallion, grazing in the backyard. Before I ever bought this place, I expected to have one like it someday. I cut out pictures of ranch style houses and kept them in my dream book. Every chance I got I would go to Santa Fe and wander through the square, soaking up the Southwestern look and reveling in it, even though at the time everything I owned was

Southern California baby boomer. That is why it is very comfortable for me here now, in this brown stucco Santa Fe–style house built around a courtyard. The light fixture above me is an old wagon wheel with clay pots inset between the spokes. It dangles from a ten foot chain set between huge wooden beams. It was designed by the same artisan who created the light fixtures for my favorite hotel in Santa Fe. What a coincidence. The light fixture came with the house. This place, a total blessing and miracle from a financial point of view, did not come as a surprise. My heart expected to live in a place like this one day, and that expectation helped create the ultimate reality of the event.

When my mother moved to Sedona in her seventies, she told us that she expected that she had five more healthy years left to live, and she wanted to live them up there. Five years have now come and gone, and we kids are awaiting her word on her next action plan. She and I were sitting on her deck reading the paper together one morning and she said, "I know I said I was going to live here only five years, but since I've been reading the obituary pages I've noticed something. The people in Sedona live a very long time. Most of them don't die until they are ninety something. So, I'm revising my plan. I'm going to live here another ten years. I may have more healthy years left than I thought!"

In a seminar I attended recently we were instructed to stand facing the speaker, and then swing around and point to a place on the wall behind us, marking it in our mind. Then we were told to face forward again. This time we were instructed to visualize ourselves turning 30 percent farther than we had the last time, but we were to do so still keeping our feet facing forward. When the instructor said "Go!" we swung around, and indeed, in my case, I had gone much farther past the point on the wall than I originally thought I could. We changed our expectations, and in so doing, increased our performance. Our new expectation became the prophecy.

There is a huge but subtle difference in attitude between hoping something will happen and expecting something to happen.

Being somewhat of a romantic I found the story of Barbra Streisand's meeting of James Brolin, and their subsequent marriage, both touching and prophetic. Although she had been divorced for more than two decades, Barbra had been directing and producing a movie about a woman who finally meets the love of her life. She even named and sang the film's theme song "I Finally Found Someone." (If a song isn't a prayer then I don't know what is.) She met James Brolin the night the movie was completed. Now tell me her energy in making the film had not helped carve a path of goodness to her door. She was declaring her expectation and intention all over the place, and God heard her and responded.

Jesus told a story about ten wedding attendants. Five kept their lamps lit in anticipation of the bridegroom's arrival at any moment, while five let their lamps go out. When the bridegroom finally showed up, those who had quit expecting him, and were thus unprepared, got left behind. (Matthew 25: 1-13)

I now have four dogs at the ranch which I adopted from Animal Rescue: a yellow Lab named Chula, a black lab/pointer mix named Joshua, a cocker spaniel named Nash, and a mini golden retriever mix named Beauty. Apparently, one of the most exciting events in the life of these dogs is when I go out each morning to feed the horses. They jump and wrestle and leap about my legs, competing for my attention and doing everything in their power to hinder my progress so I will stop and pet them.

However, my focus is on feeding the horses, and Joshua became the first to figure that out. While the other dogs are whining and begging for me to pet them, he runs ahead and climbs up onto the hay, situating himself precisely within arm's reach. And then he eagerly waits for me to arrive. He does not bark or whine or compete for my attention, even though he craves it more than the others. Because of where and how he positions himself, he is always the first dog to get the "full on" hug and kiss of the day. He expects me to pet him, and I do.

Jesus taught us again and again to ask with expectation. Recently I met a young man from Harlem who was on a full scholarship to a prestigious university. He didn't have the clothes or the transportation or even lunch money to go for his interview, but he just started asking everyone he knew for help. Sure enough, he made it. When I asked him how he did it, he said, "I got up in the morning and made a list of all the people I knew, and I said to myself, 'What can they say, but YES!' "

"If you ask your Father to give you a fish, do you expect a serpent?" Jesus asked. *(Matthew 7:10)*

I never can read this scripture without recalling something that happened in one of my mother's Bible study groups. It seems that "Amanda," the person in charge of the Sunday lesson, had a love of theater. When it came time for her to read this scripture to the group, she was prepared. She stood up, holding behind her back a brown paper bag. With great dramatic flair she boomed, "If you ask your Father to give you a fish, would you expect Him to give you THIS?!" Suddenly she pulled a long green rubber snake out of the bag and threw it into the group. Mom now refers to this scripture as "Matthew 911" because the paramedics had to be called in. One of the "non–snake-expecting" students fell backwards in her chair and cut her arm on the chair of another student who was exiting, stage left. (Alas, the group did not seem to appreciate Amanda's recognition of the importance of visual aids. She now has to go through a security check before she can even enter the classroom.)

Perhaps it is a good time to ask ourselves if we are really expecting our prayers to be answered, or are just hoping that they will be. Are we going to fall over in our chair when God pulls a miracle out of the bag? I can't help but think, the above example excepted, that most of us would be better prepared for snakes. We expect bad things to happen, and are shocked when good things do.

(I still sometimes use the word "Unbelievable!" when a miracle occurs. This shows that I have not yet attained Advanced Prophet Status.)

When I was on my book tour for *Jesus in Blue Jeans*, the host of a television show asked me what new books I was working on. When I told him that I was working on a book about prophecy, he asked if I was a prophet. I smiled and said, yes. He leaned toward me earnestly and said, "What is going to happen to me?" I smiled and asked him, "Well, what do you expect to have happen?" He said, "I haven't really thought about it." "Then I can't help you," I said, still smiling. "If you don't care enough about the future to have *any* expectation, then I can't give you one."

Nature abhors a vacuum, but God loves a positive "expector."

Not too long ago a young man announced in the national media on a Wednesday that he was going to get married that Friday at 10:00 A.M. in a certain setting. Nothing unusual about that, except he didn't have a bride—or even know anybody who could bring him one. Yet he was so sure that one would show up that he had purchased his tuxedo, tickets for the honeymoon, and planned for the reception. The news went out over the wire and sure enough, the day before, a beautiful redhead showed up and said that she knew she was the one. Friday afternoon their wedding pictures went out over the same wire that two days before had helped bring in the bride. That man's expectation became his prophecy.

I love reading the book of Acts—especially chapter 19. In this particular chapter Jesus had already ascended into heaven, and there was a group of new and eager apostles casting out demons and doing all sorts of miraculous works.

"So remarkable were the miracles worked by God at Paul's hands that handkerchiefs or aprons which had touched him were taken to the sick, and they were cured of their illnesses, and the evil spirits came out of them."

But some itinerant Jewish exorcists, too, tried pronouncing the name of the Lord Jesus over people who were possessed by evil spirits. They used to say, "I adjure you by the Jesus whose spokesman is Paul." Among those who did this were seven sons of Sceva, a Jewish chief priest. The evil spirit replied, "Jesus I recognize, and Paul I know about, but *who are you?" (Acts 19: 13-15)*

Oooooo! What an insult—not even to be recognized by the "pesky varmints." The demons were saying to those phony sons of Sceva that their names weren't even on their list!

This story belongs in the chapter on expectation because if you have no real desire, no true expectation of your own, you are empty. "I would that you were hot or cold, but because you are only lukewarm I will spit you out of my mouth." *(Revelations 3:16)*

What do you want? What do you expect? These are the hallmarks of true prophets. They expect what they say to come true.

Questions:

1. What do you expect in your life? Be specific.

_____

_____

2. What could you do to physically demonstrate your full expectation that your prayers will be answered? For example, a child who is praying for a puppy might begin reading books about dogs, or putting a can of dog food into the shopping cart, even though the parent seems to be saying no to the idea.

_____

_____

3. How can you create a physical space for the answered prayer to flow into? For instance, if you want a new wardrobe you might give away clothes you no longer need or wear, making room in the closet for the new outfit you expect. The child wanting the puppy might prepare a bed for it in the utility room, in anticipation of its arrival.

_____

_____

Meditation

Dear Lord,
Just as Noah fully expected your word to prove true, I am today
buying lumber to begin my ark. I will not listen to my neighbors'
derisive laughter or let their parties or shopping excursions distract
me from my expectation of incredible things to come. I run ahead
to meet you. I make a place for you in my life, and I expect you to
meet me there. Help me be aware that expectation carves a path to
my door.
  Amen

The Prophecy of Culture

*R*andom House Webster's College Dictionary lists some of the definitions of culture as: "The sum total of ways of living built up by a group of human beings and transmitted from one generation to another: a particular form or stage of civilization, as that of a nation or period; the behaviors or beliefs of a particular social, ethnic, or age group."

Cultural conditioning tells us what we believe, and thus dictates how we behave. As anyone who travels can tell you, not to be aware of a culture's particular traditions and values can be deadly.

It can also get you thrown out of a restaurant.

My friend Mel and I went to a newly opened ethnic restaurant in San Diego, excited to sit by the waterfall and eat some exotic new food. When the meal was delivered, however, it was so spicy that neither of us could eat it. Motioning the waiter over to our table, Mel kindly pointed out that the dish was too spicy, and asked the manager to replace it with something else. Suddenly the waiter pointed at the door and yelled, "I am the manager. And I won't allow a woman to complain about our cooking. Get out—you and your friend—and never come back!" Stunned by the sudden outburst, we found ourselves being shown the door.

One day some of my friends in the National Association of Women Business Owners were describing some of our worst "service" encounters. One woman, a doctor, shared that she had recently had a service station attendant come screaming out at her from behind the register when she asked him to count the change again. When she protested his rude words and actions, he yelled, "Woman, you mean nothing to me! Now go!" He was of the same ethnic group as the waiter who had thrown me and my friend out of the restaurant.

In one more encounter which proves the limiting factors a culturally engrained prejudice can provide, I was driven to New York's La Guardia airport by a sullen and dourfaced cab driver. I had to hoist my own luggage into the trunk while he stood there, and when I asked him about a New York landmark, he turned up the radio and ignored both my question, and me, the rest of the trip.

When we reached the airport I gave him a very small tip. He took the money, which was in a wad of cash, and evidently counted it as he began to drive away. He hadn't gone twenty feet when he slammed the cab into reverse, nearly running me down. He took my money and hurled it onto the sidewalk, yelling at the top of his lungs that I had insulted him. With that he jumped back into the cab and took off. He, also, was of the same ethnic background as the waiter and the service attendant.

I am not suggesting that rudeness is limited to one culture, but it seems apparent that in this particular culture women are never supposed to challenge men, no matter what their status. To them, gender always trumps social standing. Now I ask you, how far can these men go in a country where women are held in high esteem and generally given equal rights and opportunities? We were a doctor, a multimillion-dollar insurance agent, and a best-selling author, being "put in our place" by a waiter, a gas station attendant, and a cab driver, all because of cultural conditioning. These men's cultural conditioning is going to prophesy a limited future for them in America, unless they learn to behave differently.

In the film *Life Is Beautiful* two school teachers are discussing the merits of a math problem being taught in German elementary schools. "If cripples cost the state an extra four marks a day, and there are approximately 300,000 cripples in the German school system, how many marks would the government save by eliminating all the cripples?" The audience in the theater gasped as the school teachers continue to debate over dessert whether it should be a simple multiplication problem or a subtraction problem, totally overlooking the heinous message the "problem" was intending to convey. "Eliminate cripples. Save money." This type of teaching, insinuated into a culture, is what helped allow an entire nation to mindlessly eliminate cripples, doctors, writers, teachers, artists, Jews, and other "deviants" in the gas chamber. The German culture of the 1930s and '40s condoned a sense of racial superiority and thus prophesied a holocaust, and their own destruction.

Jesus told the story of the good Samaritan, who troubled himself on behalf of a Jew who had been beaten and left to die in a ditch. By breaking with the custom that forbid interracial contact, the Samaritan not only saved the Jew's life—he also became an example of someone rising above a cultural prejudice in order to prophesy a different future for the abandoned Jew.

I often think about the tree rings in a fallen tree which indicated when the seasons were good, and when they were bad, or the layers of sediment seen when a mountain is sliced to make a road—soil of different colors and stripes which show what went into making that mountain, one layer at a time.

We will, each of us, be laid down in the dust that was our time. Just as our parents belonged to the generation that was shaped by the Roaring '20s, the Depression, and World War II, our generation has been shaped by the Vietnam war, the rise of feminism, and the issue of civil rights, gay rights, and pro-choice versus pro-life. We have boomed our way into times of tremendous personal wealth without any collective sacrifice. We can now gather and disseminate information around the globe with the touch of a button on our home computers. How has this culture of ours shaped our thinking, and thus prophesied our future?

A friend of mine shared that he loves the verse about the death of King David. It reads "Now the acts of David the king, first and last, behold, they are written in the book of Samuel the seer, and in the book of Nathan the prophet . . . with all his reign and his might, and the times that went over him, and over Israel, and over all the kingdoms of the countries." *(I Chronicles 29:29-30)* What that verse is saying is that David was a man of his time who served his time, and having done that, died.

We are each born into a time—made up of cultural conditioning, opportunities, training, and prejudices. These layers which exist in and around us can help prophesy our success, or our failure. The key is whether we discern their value and their challenges, and respond.

Questions:

1. How would you identify your particular culture? What are its components?

_____

_____

2. Which of these components are limiting you?

_____

_____

3. Which of these components can help free you?

_____

_____

4. What dangerous trends do you see in our society, which, if left unchecked, can prophesy a negative outcome for many?

_____

_____

Meditation

Dear Lord,
I am a person in the times, and of the times. Help me be your
voice in this culture, and rise above any prejudices which might
hinder me or others. Give me the courage to be a Good
Samaritan, rising above limiting cultural conditioning to display
the love of God.
   Amen.

The Prophecy of Protest

$\mathcal{M}$uch of what the Old Testament prophets did was protest. They were often called to protest the direction that the nation's leadership was taking, calling them to task for erring from their stated intent to follow God. On those occasions when the protest was heeded, the nation was saved. (The city of Nineveh, for example, heeded the warnings and protests of Jonah, and changed its fate.) More often than not, however, the protests went unheeded, and the protesters were met with something much worse than disrespect. This paradigm was so obvious that Jesus often spoke about it.

"Oh Jerusalem, Jerusalem, the one who kills the prophets and stones those who are sent to her!" *(Luke 16:34)* And again in Matthew he says, "Blessed are you when they revile and persecute you, and say all kinds of evil against you falsely for my sake. Rejoice and be exceedingly glad, for great is your reward in heaven, for so they persecuted the prophets who were before you."*(Matthew 5:11 KVJ)*

The prophet's main duty is always to tell the truth, regardless of the cost. And the reward will often be persecution.

We have all seen dramatic evidence in our own times of protesters who charted a new course for nations. Nelson Mandela protested the policy of apartheid, with the reward of twenty-seven years in prison. Ultimately, however, his protests were heard and heeded, and a nation was changed.

Who among us can ever forget the sight of the young Chinese student facing down a tank in Tiananmen Square? This young man, carrying a shopping bag and simply trying to cross the square, was apparently so overwhelmed with the injustice of the scene that he stopped and dared the tank to run him over. When the tank tried to go around him he altered his course and again placed himself squarely in its path. China is trudging, slowly, reluctantly, but inevitably, toward democracy. I believe this would not have happened, and will not happen, without the prophets of protest.

Jesus often refers to us as sheep, and this metaphor is based on observation. We tend to be so passive at times, following the herd, rarely looking up from the blades of grass in front of us. Yet there is much good to be gained by lifting up our heads and seeing where the herd is going, and protesting if the direction seems dangerous.

Protest doesn't always have to mean taking up a picket sign or going to prison. Sometimes it can simply mean stating your position clearly and articulately in such a way that it is understood.

Needing to enlarge my office space in California, I gave thirty days notice to my tenant, a CPA who was rarely there, and had only a desk, two chairs, a phone, fax, copier, and a file cabinet. He and I had a prior discussion about possibly sharing the space, but as our company was growing so rapidly it became obvious that we needed every square foot. So I asked Dee to send out a nice letter and a notice, which she did.

What we received was a surprising firestorm of protest. The tenant was very upset about the thirty-day notice, even though he was on a month to month lease, and was in fact requesting sixty days. This seemed unreasonable to me, in light of the lease, and I asked Dee to extend the notice to forty-five days, and felt that would be generous. Suddenly, I hear a knock on my door, and in walks Bill, redfaced and quite upset. I asked him to sit down, offered him a glass of water (my specialty) and then said, "Obviously you are upset about this. I don't understand why. Why don't you tell me why you can't meet the terms of our agreement?" He then proceeded to tell me what was going on in his life. He was scheduled to take a vacation that month—his first in four years. His main client had suddenly died in a foreign country, and four people were now going to contest the will. He was considering moving his operation up to LA, where most of his work was anyway, and he was in the middle of doing a production budget for a group in Hollywood which needed the statistics immediately. I could tell that this man was about to have a heart attack, so I said, "Now I understand your position. From my viewpoint, all I saw was that you had a desk, two chairs, and a file cabinet, and I'm thinking 'What can be so hard about moving that? There's plenty of other office space around.' " I granted him his sixty-day extension, even though it meant I had to postpone our plans.

What if he had not come to me, but instead tried to comply with my request and ended up having a heart attack? His protest changed an outcome that had previously been put in writing (the closest thing we get to stone).

In a speech I once gave entitled "Ten Ways to Get a Raise," two of the points have to do with raising your voice and raising your hand. If you don't like the way something is going, raise your voice about it. And if you know the answer to a problem, raise your hand.

As prophets we are called to do both.

Just because something has always been done a certain way, does not mean it is *God's* way. Just because everyone else is doing something, does not mean *you* should. And just because protest seems like a very "unsheeplike" thing to do, doesn't mean that God isn't calling you to do it. After all, what other voice does God have but yours?

Mordecai warned Esther about the importance of her protesting the king's decree. As you might recall, the king had gotten drunk one night and was persuaded by an evil, jealous man named Haman to issue a decree to kill all the Jews. The king even signed the decree with his seal, which meant it was immutable. Esther's job was now to go to the king, and essentially protest this policy. There were only two catches. One—the king didn't know Esther was a Jew, and two—anyone who went to the king without being called was immediately killed without question. You can perhaps undestand Esther's hesitancy to take on the role of heroine. Yet Mordecai, her uncle, warns her, "Do not think in your heart that you will escape in the king's palace any more than all the other Jews. For if you remain completely silent at this time, relief and deliverance will arise for the Jews from another place, but you and your father's house will perish. Yet who knows whether you have come to the kingdom for such a time as this?" *(Esther 4: 13)*

God knows exactly who and where you are. What are you being called to protest? Do you think the tanks of injustice will run over everyone else and leave you unscathed, just because you chose to sit in the spectator section? What if your only purpose is to be a voice?

Have you ever had one of those dreams where someone grabs

you in the dark and you are so terrified that you can't even scream? Psychologists say it is a common dream, especially for women. Could it be due to the fact that women are often grabbed in the dark, and also perhaps because we are not sure of the importance of our own voices?

The guards handled her roughly as they hauled her off to jail. "Get in here, you troublemaker" growled the jailer as turned his back on her and locked the door. The following day she was led into court. "For your act of civil disobedience, you are hereby fined $100," said the judge as the gavel came down. She stood up, faced the judge and said, "I will never pay a dollar of your unjust penalty." Her crime had been voting in an election. Her name: Susan B. Anthony, a Quaker who had also advocated temperance, an end to slavery, and education for all children. She had come up with the theory that the United States Constitution, properly interpreted, already gave women the right to vote, so in 1871 she and fifteen other women persuaded an electioneer to cast their ballots. Fifty years later, the Nineteenth Amendment was passed, allowing women the right to vote. It was known as the Susan B. Anthony amendment. She protested, and her protest became prophetic.

Dietrich Bonhoeffer was a young, passionate theologian in Austria during the time of Hitler's rise to power. As a fair-haired specimen of physical beauty, he easily could have been considered one of Hitler's examples of excellence, and lived an unthreatened life. Yet Bonhoeffer used his platform as a professor of theology to rail against Hitler's evil philosophies which were infiltrating and infecting the consciousness of Austria and Germany alike. It is said that Bonhoeffer, a man of God, was so appalled about Hitler's rise to power he actually planned to assassinate him. His plan was discovered, and he was thrown in prison for many years. Dietrich Bonhoeffer was passionately protesting social ills, and doing everything in his power to change them. Shouldn't this be the true practice of theology?

I am struck by the many pastors, priests, and theologians who have nothing to say about the true evils which still fill our land— racism, sexism, and the reviling of outsiders. They bury their heads in rows and rows of dusty books and teach us the way it used to be, never catching a glimpse of how "things ain't how they're supposed to be NOW."

I'm guilty of this. I don't speak up nearly enough when I see a wrong in society. I tell myself it is because I have chosen to light candles rather than curse darkness, and that is true. But am I really doing enough? Do I think just one voice won't do it?

Recently in my home town an election for a local city official was determined by one vote. It wasn't that the tally was 313,462 to 313,461. It was that the tally was 1-0. One candidate received one vote, and the other got none. What makes this story even more hilarious and revealing is that the candidate who won the election by one vote didn't even know he was running. And ultimately, he was disqualified because he did not live in the district he was running to represent. This meant that the person who won by default had received *zero* votes. This city has a population of 765,000 people, which is in a border area encompassing nearly two million people. The challenges facing the region are legion. Yet in the election for a Democratic party supervisor, the total people who cared amounted to one—one woman who left work early and drove clear across town to drop her ballot in a box at the fire station. The guy who won by default hadn't even bothered to vote for himself.

Does this story remind you in any way of your situation—at work, at home, in your church or synagogue? Are you allowing other people, or processes, to determine your future based on default?

I worked in a congressman's office one summer when I was seventeen, and part of my task was reading the mail that came in and keeping a tally of the letters, sorting them into "pro" or "con" piles on issues. One letter was usually counted as representing two hundred and fifty voters. I recently learned from a network official that in broadcasting one letter is equated to represent ten thousand viewers. A woman who was a columnist at *USA Today* said that the ratio was considered the same for the newspaper. Clearly, those who protest can shift and shape policy far more than those who do not.

Amnesty International has an Urgent Action Network which notifies members to write, call, fax and e-mail their messages of protest to government officials on behalf of prisoners in life-threatening situations. One such successful protest involved Dr. Fathi Subuth, a university professor in the Palestinian Authority, who was arrested because he taught a class on critical thinking. During his arrest he was tortured and held without legal cause. Halfway through Dr. Subuth's detention, an Amnesty delegate met with a colonel in the Palestinian Preventive Security Service. At that time, the Colonel reported that the had already received 3,500 letters asking for Dr. Subuth's release. Upon his release Dr. Subuth expressed deep gratitude to Amnesty members for their work on his behalf. Their protest wrote a new future for him, as it has for so many prisoners of all walks and countries whose only crime is protesting authori-

ties in power. Can a letter of protest make a difference? Dr. Subuth knows it can.

USA Today recently carried an article entitled "Out On a Limb
to Fight for Trees." It profiled a woman named Julia Butterfly Hill,
who had taken a few belongings and made a nest two hundred feet
up in a giant redwood tree to protest the destruction of hundreds of
acres of redwood trees in Oregon. She'd been a waitress with no
real vision for life—just getting by, until a car accident and a near
fatal brain injury gave her a new perspective. Somehow she came
out of the hospital with a passion to help save the world. Not the
people in it, per se, so much as the trees on it. And not just all
the trees—but specifically the trees in the redwood forest.

At the time of this article she had been perched in the tree
for four hundred sixty-five days. Her purpose was to call attention to the ongoing destruction of the giant trees—trees which
once covered two million acres in an expanse that stretched from
Oregon to Big Sur.

Labeled by many as a "radical tree hugger," Hill and others
in Earth First! claim, among other things, that it was exorbitant
to pay a Houston financier $50,000 an acre for land that had cost
him only $3,000 an acre to purchase from Pacific Lumber.
Charles Hurwitz, the financer, triggered years of protest by or-
dering that the redwood forest cutting be tripled in order to pay
off the high interest junk bonds he had used for the takeover of
the lumber company.

Prompted in part by Hill's fifteen month vigil in the lonely
tree she has named "Luna," the Federal Government has recently negotiated the purchase of 7,500 acres from Hurwitz to
maintain as a preserve.

Hill asked also that Luna, her tree, be spared. The lumber company has so far denied her request, saying "We don't negotiate with people who are breaking the law."

Interestingly enough, Julia Butterfly Hill was recently named one of *Good Housekeeping* magazine's "Most Admired Woman of the Year."

All the interesting women I know are a little bit "outlaws." Author Harriet Rubin writes in her book *Princessa: Machiavelli for Woman*, "One day we will learn that we were not sent here to support people who are running the world as it is. We were sent here to rearrange it."

A woman's voice can carry ten miles in still water, according to a study done on sound. Julia Butterfly Hill's voice carried all the way to Washington, D.C., some two thousand miles away.

Perhaps the lesson is that our voice will carry farther from the treetops than it will in still water.

Jesus said "A person does not light a candle and put it under a bushel—but on a stand, so that its light can be seen for miles." *(Matthew 5:15)*

Visibility. Protest. We must make our voices heard.

America began in protest—and may she always remain. When we lose opposing voices, then we will surely have lost our way.

The prophecy of protest. We are called to shape the future, using our voice.

Questions:
1. What situation do you know you need to protest—
   a. at work

b. at home

_____

c. in your church

_____

d. in your community

_____

2. If knew your voice was counted as representing ten thousand others, would you use it in protest more often?

_____

_____

3. Name six protesters in history that you admire, and why.

_____

_____

4. State what they protested, and the outcome of their protests.

_____

_____

5. Why can protest be prophetic?

_____

_____

Meditation

Dear Lord,
You gave me a voice so I could use it. Let me not be a mere
spectator in this life. Let me stand up and protest what is not right.
Let me be your voice that helps lead the crowds back to you—your
love, your compassion, your calling. Let me always be aware that
in this world, you have no voice to use but ours.

Amen

The Prophecy of Play

"Pause a while and know that I am God."

Psalm 46:10

$\mathcal{M}$any of us have the idea that God is very serious and ponderous and solemn. Yet a look at creation reveals an undercurrent of joyfulness and playfulness that is also God's reflection.

In the book *Chicken Soup for the Pet Lover's Soul* a writer shares that when he was a tour guide in the wild he was startled to see a buffalo come running down a hill and slide spreadeagle across the icy surface of a lake. Thinking that was an accident, he said to his friend standing beside him, "That is one dumb buffalo." The friend, who was the senior guide, smiled and said, "Watch." The buffalo went trudging back up the hill, followed now by two other buffalo, and they proceeded to charge one by one down the hill and slide crazily across the ice in some sort of random buffalo ice hockey game. Who would have thought that buffalos know how to play? Who put that spirit in them?

Throughout the Old Testament God is known as the God of Abraham, Isaac, and Jacob. I once a heard a sermon to the effect that these three patriarchs each represent an aspect of God. Abraham represents the total and utter faith God requires of us, Jacob represents how even a conniver can become a great person of God, and Isaac represents the miraculous grace of God, where everything is simply given to us.

Isaac was the son born to Abraham and Sarah when they were

well past their childbearing years. "Sarah shall bear you a son; and you are to name him Isaac, which means 'laughter.' " *(Genesis 17:19)*

Unlike many people in the Bible, Isaac led an easy life. He was a good and obedient son who loved to walk in the fields and meditate. He had a wife named Rebekah whom he absolutely and totally adored. Everything he did was blessed. Isaac became a man of great wealth and prosperity, no matter where he settled. Apart from a few challenges by the Philistines here and there, Isaac had few worries, and died an old and happy man. Isaac is proof that a life lived in God doesn't have to be hard. Sometimes, it can be easy, and actually fun.

If you believe that Isaac was loved by God even though he didn't do anything heroic to earn it, and if you believe that even buffalos can devise games to amuse themselves, it should come as no surprise that God often delivers messages to people in play. The spirit of God can be as playful as a kitten, and recently that was brought home to me when I was feeling very sorry for myself.

I was lying on the couch in the sunroom, totally silent under doctor's orders. My vocal cords were swollen and nonfunctional. I had just returned from a month on the road doing back to back speaking engagements, and the fatigue factor was in full swing. On this particular day I was indulging myself in just how very bad I felt.

Facing another week of intense travel, I decided to pull a Jeremiah, which is a "woe is me, why don't you just take me now, Lord, and spare me further agony" litany. The thought ocurred to me in a sort of playful fantasy, what if I just died, right there on the couch, and never had to pack another suitcase again. People would have to pack for me. They would come and carry me out on a clean white stretcher . . . they would even have to clean off my desk. (I was really getting into it.) Just then the phone rang.

A voice on the line said "Is this Ms. Jones?" "Yes it is," I whispered, highly annoyed because I didn't recognize the voice, and my phone number is unlisted—to screen out such unwanted calls. "Who are you?" I demanded. "Ms. Jones, we here at Memory Gardens are pleased to inform you that you have just been selected to win a free burial plot . . ." I paused for a moment trying to comprehend the irony of this call. "Thank you," I whispered in a much nicer tone, "but I won't be needing it after all." I had to laugh. God was calling me on my bluff. He really *does* have my number.

> O Lord, You have searched me and known me.
> You know my sitting down and my rising up;
> You understand my thought afar off.
> You comprehend my path and my lying down,
> and are acquainted with all my ways.
> For there is not a word on my tongue,
> but behold, O Lord, You know it altogether.
>
> —*Psalm 139:1–4 King James Version*

America was heavily influenced by the Puritans, who thought and taught that idle hands were the devil's playground. Play has not been highly regarded in our culture. If productivity has become the golden calf we worship, then people who are playing can't be productive, right? Wrong. Witness the results of Southwest Airlines, whose CEO, Herb Kelleher, fosters and encourages a spirit of play among the workforce. Once, when facing a lawsuit by a rival company, Herb said, "Aw, shucks. This is Texas. Why don't we just arm wrestle over it, and whoever wins, wins." To the astonishment of the media, the opposing CEO agreed, and a wrestling match was held. Herb won, and that settled it.

When I was on a Southwest flight recently, as everyone was being seated, the pilot announced over the intercom, "Hi, folks. This is your captain speaking. As you all are getting settled, could you do us a favor and pick a seat by the window? That way we'll look full to the Delta flight crew over there."

Southwest stock has risen 2,300 percent since its inception twenty years ago, and it has the number one customer satisfaction record in the industry. Can playfulness prophesy success? In this case, yes.

The young man was about to be kicked out of high school for his low grades in math. His mother had told his father that she feared that he would end up living with them forever. His father took him aside and said, "Son, you have to stop daydreaming. I've enrolled you in a vocational school to study plumbing." The young man brushed his hair out of his eyes and said, "Father, don't you understand? Imagination is everything." That night he dreamed that he was sledding, and in his dream the light follwed his sled and became a rainbow. His interpretation of that dream led to the theory of relativity. Albert Einstein always left time to stare out the window and play. His playtime fantasies helped explain how time exists. Einstein also said that if certain events could be foretold, then time was not a continuum, but a field of undefinable shape—ever moving, ever dancing. Like a boy on a sled, perhaps, propelled by a rainbow into the light.

In a recent article in *Time* magazine there was a full page discussion about a study which suggests that our children are overscheduled, overworked and running out of time for fun. Children's leisure time, which in 1981 ranked as taking up 40 percent of their lives, now only occupies 25 percent of their time, and that percentage is slipping. Unstructured play encourages independent thinking and allows the young to negotiate their relationships with their peers, says T. Bery Brazelton, a pediatrician at Harvard Medical School. "Yet nowadays children ages three to twelve spend only twelve hours a week engaged in this activity. If we don't pay attention to this," he warns, "we are going to create obsessive-compulsive adults."

In her book *Beyond Love and Work: Why Adults Need to Play*, author Lenore Terr, M.D., clinical professor of psychiatry at the University of California, writes that "people who preserve their sense of fun are better equipped to solve problems, think creatively, and manage stress."

Dan Sullivan teaches a course for successful entrepreneurs entitled The Strategic Coach. I remember so well sitting in my first session of the course, surrounded by highly motivated overachievers. When asked why they were there, each person shared his or her reasons. The man sitting across from me in the sharing circle opened his shirt to reveal a six-inch-long scar on his chest. "This is why I came," he said. "So I won't need more surgery later." The most amazing and difficult concept that Dan teaches these super-earners is the importance of "free days." His definition of "free day" is so stringent that if you look at a file, make a phone call that pertains to business, or even play golf with a client, you have turned your free day into a buffer or focus day and you can't count it. He makes each person in the course commit to taking at least forty free days per year. What his research has shown him, he says, is that people tend to be more alert, creative, and capable of handling life's complexities after taking time to play. He further asserts that God played a long time before creating the world, and on the seventh day he took a glorious free day, and turned off the phone.

In my book *Jesus, CEO* I recount how often Jesus played with his followers—at parties, weddings, dinners, banquets all over Jerusalem. "The kingdom of heaven is like a banquet," Jesus says in *Matthew 22:2*. In heaven, people are havng a good time. In other words, joy and laughter are the natural state.

In contrast, we on earth often think that everything must be cut and dried, particularly if we are trying to accomplish something big. Yet in nature, a lack of warmth can lead to disastrous consequences. Avalanches are caused when the temperature is so cold and dry that the snowflakes fail to bond with one another. Without some sunshine and a little softness around the edges the flakes do not hold together. One sudden sneeze or any other slightest provocation can have disastrous effects. Have you ever been in a setting—at work or home—like that?

Jesus made sure there were plenty of warm and bonding times with his disciples. They could remember the glow of the candlelight at the table as they sat together and sang songs, or recounted stories about the day, or watched him play with the children. Jesus loved to party and play. "I, the Messiah, feast and drink." *(Matthew 11:19)*

In a recent article, movie star Kathy Bates shared a story she'd heard. It seems a newly hired city orchestra leader took his title and his fame quite seriously. He spent all his time in his dressing room, or with the well-to-do in the city, and failed to show up for the staff parties which were common to orchestra members.

When the time came for his big debut, he fluffed back his black coat tails, bowed to the audience, turned sternly to the orchestra, and gave the opening drop of the baton. Nothing happened. Startled and embarrassed, he tapped the music stand loudly three times, raised his baton and, with a strict snap of his wrist, brought it down again. Nothing. Stepping back with his head tilted in fury, the orchestra leader learned a lesson when a cellist finally stood up and said, "Mr. Conductor, this is just a reminder that no sound comes out of that baton of yours." All work and no play made Jack look like a fool in front of his colleagues.

Do you know why God made the seas? For the whales to play in.

> O Lord, how manifold are Your works!
> In wisdom You have made them all.
> The earth is full of Your possessions—
> This great and wide sea,
> in which are innumerable teeming things,
> Living things both small and great.
> There the ships sail about;
> There is that Leviathan
> Which You have made to play there.
> —*Psalm 104:24-26 King James Version*

I will never forget standing in front of the arctic exhibit at Sea World and watching a little puffin play. Jumping off the shore into the water, this delightful little handpainted-looking bird would dive and then twirl and flip and swim backwards underwater as fast as she could. Then she would suddenly burst up into the air, settle on the surface for a moment, and then dive again, chasing the bubbles that it had created. I stood transfixed for fifteen minutes watching that puffin display every move it was capable of making, reveling in each one. And I just knew that God was standing there with me—the two of us just watching it.

Perhaps play is the purest form of worship, for it has no agenda other than delighting in the sheer, immeasurable joy of being alive.

Worship puts us in touch with the divine, and when we are in touch with the divine we rise to our highest and our best. And this is prophecy.

With all our technological understanding and advancements, when we perpetuate an atmosphere of pompous "seriousity," we are like the piano player, who after years of practice was told, "The training in your fingers has unfortunately only served to more loudly demonstrate your ignorance of sound." Is it possible to hit all the right notes and still not put forth the right sound? Anyone who has been to a piano recital knows this is true. It's true in life, too. I say in my book *Grow Something Besides Old: Seeds for a Joyful Life* that "If you have to watch every step you take, the path you are on is too narrow."

At one of the Path Facilitator Training Seminars, we were privileged to have in our midst a man named Roberto. A highly placed executive in the international offices of a Fortune 500 company, he had come to the seminar to clarify his personal mission statement. After going through the formulas and exercises for the first day and a half, he said he was still frustrated by what he had written down, and wasn't sure whether he was going to get a clear mission statement at all. Finally, I asked him what he wanted to be about in the world. He stood up and said, "I want to make Jesus real through fun and laughter." There was a silence in the room which I have come to recognize as the Holy Spirit confirming what has just been spoken, and I said, "Roberto, that's it!" "What's it?" "That is your mission statement!" "Say it for me," he said. "Your mission is to make Jesus real through fun and laughter." There was another long silence, and then he threw his head back and laughed the purest, longest, deepest laugh I have ever heard. The people in the room spontaneously leapt to their feet and clapped and cheered. What could be more beautiful, meaningful, or necessary in this world than "making Jesus real through fun and laughter."

The little children were eager to reach Jesus. They began crowding all around him, wanting perhaps to sit in his lap or maybe have him ruffle the hair on their heads. Their parents just wanted him to pray over them, but the children wanted to play. One of them might have called out from the crowd, "Come run with me, Jesus. Run!" But the disciples rebuked them, saying this great man was too busy to play with children. Then Jesus turned and said, "Let the little children come to Me, and do not forbid them, for of such is the Kingdom of Heaven." *(Matthew 19: 13–14)*

This concept of how play becomes prophecy is so important to me because I owe my very life to it.

The young woman couldn't believe it when the phone rang, telling her that her husband had been found dead in a car up on Scenic Drive—an apparent suicide. Struggling to comprehend the incomprehensible act of taking one's life, she remembered what a tortured, artistic soul he had displayed even when they first met. His bouts of depression had not been alleviated by their move to the Southwest, and one day the despair all came crashing in on him, and he died, leaving the lovely twenty-five-year-old woman a widow with a mountain of debt.

She took two jobs to try to pay everyone off, and became a shadow of her former self. She herself had to wrestle nightly with discouragement and self-doubt. About six months later she met him—a young salesman with a twinkle in his eye who insisted that she put down her bookwork for a while and go dancing. At first she was not interested—he certainly didn't look like the marrying kind. He still lived with his mother, and those ties he wore were a little bit on the ridiculous side.

Meanwhile, another suitor had shown up on the scene. This one was rich. He owned a car dealership in town, and was enchanted by the dark-haired beauty who seemed so sad. He would ask her out a week in advance, then call an hour ahead of time and ask her what color dress she was going to wear. She would soon see him pull up in front of the boarding house, driving a car the same color as her dress, bearing a matching corsage.

When I heard Mom recounting this story I exclaimed, "Mom, that guy was rich! It sounds like he adored you!" "Yes, he did." She kind of smiled. "Then why did you marry Dad?" I asked, eager to hear a lengthy explanation. She got a faraway look in her eye and then said, "Because he made me laugh."

I can't help but wonder where I would be today if my father hadn't had that twinkle in his eye that said to a grieving "Blue Lady," "I can make you laugh again. The world is full of fun."

Do you want to prophesy? Go play, and when you do you will hear and understand the heart and mind of God.

Questions:

1. Why would God speak to us through play?

_____

_____

2. Write down your definition of what it means to "play."

_____

_____

3. How much unstructured time do you allow in your day?

_____

_____

4. Who makes you laugh the most?

_____

_____

5. How much time do you spend with that person?

_____

_____

6. When was the last time you had a really good idea? Where were you?

_____

_____

7. How could watching someone else play lead you to a prophecy about them and their future?

_____

_____

Meditation

Dear Lord,
You gave Isaac a life filled with laughter. You created animals
with a capacity for playing and enjoying your creation. Help me
take time to play, make room to play, value play as an expression
of heaven, and as a means of receiving your words.
   Amen.

Self-fulfilling Prophecies

"What I feared has come upon me."
Job 3:25
"I shall be revered in all generations."
Mary in Luke 1:40

The two scriptures on the previous page, one from Job and the other from Mary, serve to highlight the relevance of self-fulfilling prophecies. With both these people, the beliefs they held about themselves came true.

In my living room hangs a huge painting done by my friend Irene Prat. It shows a green and orange ribbon laid down over rolling sand dunes. At times the ribbon disappears behind a dune, only to reemerge on the hill behind it. At the horizon point the ribbon breaks off from the dune and gently curls into the sky.

I call the painting "Prophecy," because that's what it reminds me of. Prophecies are like ribbons of light leading us across the desert. Many times the "prophecies" leading us are our own beliefs.

We learn a lot about life through death, and some of my experience with self-fulfilling prophecies came from the deaths of those closest to me.

My father was a voracious athlete. I started to write the word "tremendous" but that would have implied that he was successful at it. He wasn't. He was simply voracious about it. He played basketball at the YMCA until Mom finally forbid it after his latest episode of getting run over by the teenagers. He played racquetball and handball and tennis and swam and turned down promotion after promotion in his company because it would have meant giving him less time for his sports. Although he did love eating ice cream by the gallon, he was very careful otherwise about his weight, and had a nice physique. People thought he was much younger than he was.

Dad had a thing about illness. He refused to acknowledge it. If you were sick, all you needed to do was work out a little harder, and you'd get better. He also could not go into hospitals, because the very smell of a hospital would make him faint. Mom said that he even fainted when they gave him a blood test before they got married. He told me one time, "Laurie, if I ever get so old that I can't play sports, please promise me that you will push me over a cliff." When the subject of death came up, he would laugh. "I am going to drop dead either playing tennis or racquetball." Sure enough, one month after his sixty-fourth birthday he was playing racquetball with a friend of his, had a massive heart attack, and dropped dead on the court. Nobody was able to revive him, although there were several doctors playing at the club at the time. Oddly enough, he had just had a physical the week before, and his doctor had told him he had the body of a man twenty years younger. I can't help but think that my father prophesied his own death.

A family friend of ours did the same thing. Madge became an avid born-again Christian right after the Charismatic movement began sweeping the country in the early '70s. A woman who was never known for much more than yelling, "Sammy, come home!" over the fence to her husband became suddenly very active in her church. I can remember my father refusing to call the Smiths' house, even though Sammy was his best tennis partner. He would say, "Laurie, will you call Sammy and see if he can play tennis?" And I'd say, "Sure, Dad, but I'd rather watch you call him." When the phone would ring Madge would answer "Smith Residence. PRAISE THE LORD!" and it used to just drive my father nuts. He would slam down the phone in exasperation, refusing to leave a message about tennis at such a heavenly household.

One day when she was in her late seventies she was in the church choir, raising her hands and singing at the top of her lungs "PRAISE THE LORD!" when she dropped dead. (Whether my father, who had already "gone on to glory," chose to cue the Lord to take her at that moment remains to be seen.) The point is, she died exactly as she had wished. She had declared to anyone who would listen that she was going to die praising the Lord.

Obviously, not everyone prophesies their own death. But belief is such a powerful thing that it can work in death, as well as life.

Motivational speaker Tony Robbins shares the phenomena of self-fulfilling prophecies with an interesting example. People who study accidents have observed that if there is a single tree or telephone pole as the only standing object on a stretch of road, people will tend to hit it when their cars spin out of control. The odds are such that there is so much open space around the trees that it would have been easier for them to miss it than hit it. One theory surfacing is that the reason people end up crashing into the tree, rather than missing it, is because the people begin to panic and say to themselves, "Don't hit the tree!" The tree becomes the object of their focus, and that's where the brain directs the body to turn. We are learning that for some reason the brain does not understand, record, or respond to the word "not." (You can corroborate this study with an informal test of your own on any group of two-year-olds.) So when we declare, "Do not hit the tree," what the brain understands is, "Do hit the tree."

I will share two of the many self-fulfilling prophecies I have personally experienced. The first one is short and simple.

In 1974 I declared in my journal that I was going to write a book called *Jesus in Blue Jeans*. Twenty-three years later, I held the published book in my hand.

Perhaps the more amazing one to me was when I wrote in my journal in 1989 that someday I was going to personally meet Mikhail Gorbachev and shake his hand. I wanted to thank him for the work he did in ending the Cold War and for helping to bring about the collapse of Communism. At the time I wrote this down I was an advertising agency owner and real estate agent who was not involved in politics at any level. I went about my business for several years, and one day I got an invitation in the mail from Mikhail Gorbachev himself, inviting me to attend the first State of the World Forum. This was a gathering of writers and students, Nobel Peace–prize winners, statesmen and women, scientists, economists, and environmentalists who were gathering to discuss the state of the world, and examine creative solutions to solve its problems.

I sat there at my desk turning over the invitation in my hand. "Okay," I thought, "I must be one of thousands of people that have been invited, but how did they get my name?" I was even more astounded to learn upon my arrival that I was being asked to serve on a panel of twenty people with Mikhail Gorbachev himself, which was to meet in one of the breakout sessions. Three months later, I was sitting at a table with Mikhail Gorbachev in the ballroom of the Fairmont Hotel, offering my opinion on world issues. After the session ended I walked five steps over to him. He stopped and smiled at me, and said (through his translator) that I had made a very valuable contribution to the discussion. I reached out my hand to thank him, then gave him a big bear hug and whispered in his ear, "Thank you for all you have done." He hugged me back and smiled the biggest smile, looking right into my eyes, and then he was ushered off to his next meeting. To this day I do not know how that committee got my name. But what I had prophesied in my journal had been fulfilled.

In my studies about human behavior over the past twenty years, I am convinced that there is no single force as powerful for human beings as "belief." It is the one thing we will die for, right or wrong. It is such a powerfully motivating force in people that it can cause us to do inhuman and inhumane things. I am also convinced that without beliefs, we are dangerously malleable. You might say that beliefs are the skeletal structure of the personality. If that structure is not properly aligned, you will have a warped and dysfunctional person. Beliefs become self-fulfilling prophecies—some of which are negative.

Not too long ago there was a television report about a family whose religious beliefs forbade them from seeking medical help for their little ten-year-old boy, who was suffering from an earache. Praying that God would heal him, they refused to take him to the doctors, and the boy finally died from a raging infection that could have been cured with antibiotics. This family's *belief* that God would punish those who disobeyed their religious edicts was stronger and more motivating than their fear that their son would die, their concern for what the authorities would do, or their concern over what the loss of this son would do to their other eight children. Their belief was stronger than their parental concern and love. Their belief in the rightness of their religion was also stronger than their faith that God would heal him. They told a reporter, "If God wants to take him, He will." This became a self-fulfilling prophecy, because of a strong, yet unhealthy, belief.

Another example of the power of belief came from an acquaintance who, despite her beauty, believed that she was not beautiful. In a constant quest for beauty and acceptance, she has had more than twenty plastic surgeries, skin abrasions, liposuctions, chin suctions, and fashion makeovers. Hearing about a new guru in Southern California, she attended a seminar where the guru taught that we are simply tied up in old belief systems that do not work, especially in regards to relationships. Part of the process of this work was having an issue come up, and then having the person examine what the belief was behind it. This sounds harmless enough, but what the guru then did was have the person erase that belief. What happened to my friend was that she became attracted to a younger man in the group. Being honest, she spoke out her attraction, and then said that her fear was that she was too old for him, and that her husband might be jealous if she had an affair with "Jim." The guru had her state each fear, and then repeat after the fear, "This is only a belief I have. It is not the truth." So, Sally's conversation went, "I think I am too old for Jim. But this is only a belief I have. It is not the truth. My husband will be jealous if I have an affair with Jim. However, this is only a belief I have. It is not the truth." Thus armed with her new non-belief system, Sally launched into an affair with Jim, and told her husband, Bill, who did indeed get upset. At the lunch I had with some friends, Sally rushed in with a Victoria's Secret exuberance, wearing a gold lamé see-through blouse and black leather pants and stiletto heels. "Didn't I tell you I was so beautiful I was dangerous?" she asked, while my friends and I just looked at her in shock. "Guess what!" she gushed. "I used to think that sex was just for marriage, but that was an old belief system. Now, I am appearing in adult erotic 'documentaries' and loving it! I have never had so much fun!" "And Bill?" asked Sue. "Oh, he's still caught up in some old belief systems about marriage," said Sally. "What about Jim?" asked Jill. "Well, Jim is constantly flirting with younger women in the seminars, but he says my jealousy is just a belief I have that no longer serves me. I did tell him I wasn't going to pay for everything anymore, even though he said I had an old belief system about there not being enough money to go around." Sue and Jill and I could scarcely believe what we were hearing. "Sally, don't you know that sex with a group of strangers is dangerous, whether or not there are cameras rolling?" "Jill," said Sally, reaching for a carrot, "that is just an old belief about disease that no longer serves me. I am having a ball!" she screamed, getting out her compact to retouch her already too heavy makeup.

We quietly left her and called the prayer line. Sally, a formerly attractive, successful, married woman was in the process of undoing her career, her marriage, her finances, and soon her health, simply because she had decided not to have any belief system at all. She had become a mass of human protoplasm with no structural means of support, other than a pair of tight leather pants and stiletto heels. Despite the unraveling of almost all her other beliefs, the pervading belief that she was not beautiful remained untouched. Her underlying negative belief about herself was becoming a self-fulfilling prophecy before our eyes.

Jesus tells the story about three servants who were each given a certain number of talents by a wealthy man. "To one he gave five talents, to another two, and to another one, to each according to his own ability." Then the wealthy man goes on a journey. The servant who received five talents went and traded with them, and made another five talents. The other servant also did some trading, and doubled what he had been given. The one who had received one talent went and dug a hole in the ground, and hid his lord's money. When the wealthy man returns to settle accounts, he finds that two of the servants had done well with their gifts. He praises both of them effusively. "Well done, good and faithful servants; you were faithful over a few things, I will make you ruler over many things. Enter into the joy of your lord." Listen, however, to what the other man believed about his lord, and what happened as a result of his belief. "Then the one who had received the one talent came and said, "Lord, I knew you to be a hard man . . . so I went and hid your talent in the ground. Look, there you have what is yours." In a graphic case of a self-fulfilling prophecy coming true, his lord answered him as a hard man would. "You wicked and lazy servant . . . take the talent from him, and give it to the one who has more." *(Matthew 25: 13–28)* The servant who expected to be treated roughly, was.

What you expect to happen, so often will.

Actor Jim Carrey, who was on the verge of bankruptcy at the time as a starving actor in Hollywood, took out a check and wrote it out to himself for the amount of ten million dollars. He dated the check three years in advance. In an amazing tale of fact following fiction, he received a contract for his third movie, in the amount of ten million dollars, almost three years to the day from when he had written it.

What we think about, we become. What we think and speak, has power.

That is the impact, and the truth, of self-fulfilling prophecies.

Questions:

1. What self-fulfilling prophecies have you expressed?

_____

_____

2. Who do you know who is living out a self-fulfilling prophecy?

_____

_____

3. What self-image do you have?

_____

_____

4. A person will always act out what they really believe. Is this statement true or false? Why?

_____

_____

5. Which is more powerful—a prophecy given to you by someone else or one which you give yourself?

_____

_____

Meditation

O Lord,
I know that I will become what I focus on. Help me to see your
image of me, and fulfill that.
    Amen.

Negative Prophecies
and How to Overcome Them

"Beware of false prophets among you."
Matthew 7:15

$\mathcal{U}$sually about one-third of the people surveyed at any of my speeches or seminars would respond that they had been given a negative prophecy rather than a positive one. Having been raised in a state and a family where "never was heard a discouraging word" I was duly inspired by the stories of people who had to fight to overcome the powerful, negative words of others.

One of my favorite activities is horseback riding in the country with my dogs running alongside. On this particular day I was riding along the riverbank with Jenny, my cocker spaniel, who by nature was usually fifty yards ahead of me, a blond blur of exploratory delight. Not seeing her in front of me, I turned and called for her. I could see her standing near some bushes. "Come on, Jenny! Come on!" I called and then turned and continued loping along. A few more seconds passed and she had not caught up to us. I turned again and saw that she was standing in the same place. She was not usually disobedient, so I turned my horse, Sunny, around and went back to where she was. "Jenny, I said come along now!" She stood stock-still. I decided to dismount and see what the problem was. She wasn't hurt or in pain, evidently, as she was wagging her tail. As I got closer I recognized the problem. She had gotten tangled up in some fishing line that had wrapped around her chest and legs and was keeping her from moving. I carefully untangled it, putting it in my pocket so it wouldn't ensnare any other little creature, and got back on my horse. Jenny took off like a blur in front of me, her race for glory now unimpeded by invisible, tangled strands.

Sometimes negative prophecies are like fishing line on a river bank that we stumble into and can't shake off by ourselves. Invisible to the naked eye, those nylon strands are just as powerful as chains. So, too, can words be which hurt or degrade or hold us back.

Richmond Mayo-Smith is a member of the Class of 1944 at Amherst College. He says, "I find it hopeful to think that the underlying cause of our difficulties may be that we are living the wrong story."

In my seminars when I ask people to recall a positive prophecy someone said about them, several people will raise their hand and ask me to come over to them. While the others are busy writing theirs down, these people ask in a whisper, "What if you can't remember ever receiving a positive prophecy?" When I would ask them to then think of a negative prophecy that someone said that affected their life, the stories would begin to flow.

Sometimes a negative prophecy is a positive prophecy turned inside out. Look at how the people in the following stories reacted to their "negative prophecies."

At age eighteen, I was working at a drug store, when I was told by the manager, "The reason we hire people like you is because you have little ambition and will be content staying in a minimum wage job. You will get married, get fat, have a lot of children, and never leave." Instead I decided to pursue my dream. I have developed programs to help those in need, be-

come active in my community and learned to deal with the
ghosts of my past. I went to college, got a degree in nursing
and two certificates in Social Work therapy. I now direct nurses
and therapists to help others learn new ways of coping with
mental illness and addiction. He is still the manager of that
drug store. —M.W.

Can it be a surprise that the manager who could offer no words
of positive support to an impressionable youth is still in the same
place? Perhaps he has never been the recipient of prophecy, good
or bad, to spur him on.

Fortunately, this man also overcame a negative prophecy
about his intellectual capabilities.

When I attended high school, the quality of teaching was not
the best. There was no challenge in the classes for me, and my
grades were poor. The principal advised me not to take college
prep courses, as I "would not succeed in college." So after high
school, I joined the Navy, then went to work in an auto parts
store and a gas station. Later I went to work in the quality
control lab of a manufacturing company, thinking this was the
best I could do. Yet on this job, I came up with several ideas
to increase production. I was promoted into production as an
assistant foreman, then to foreman of a department, and finally
to foreman of two departments with twenty-six men under
my supervision. At one point, I was asked to participate in an
IQ exam with a doctor from the University of Southern California. After the test, I was advised that I had an IQ of 138+,
and could succeed in college. Shortly after that, I quit my job,
enrolled at a junior college, graduated, went on to San Diego

State University, and graduated number two in the class of Civil Engineers. —J.B.

In this case a prophecy of nonsuccess by a respected authority led a young man to become a gas station attendant. His natural genius eventually began to exert itself, thank God, and he finally caught the attention of another authority, who told him he had an incredible IQ. With this new prophecy, this person went on to graduate number two in his class. What a telling example of the directions prophecies and predictions have over us.

I am a middle child, always the "pleaser," and was told by my high school counselor that since I was a B student in high school, I'd be average in college. I believed him and never tried hard. I always thought others were smarter and more capable than I. Yet, all my life I loathed being average. In fact, the older I get the more I loathe it.

It has taken me decades to decide that I can really achieve and be excellent at something. At the age of fifty, I received my black belt in Tae Kwon Do. I am now becoming a master potter. Each decade I am taking on a new challenge and goal. I believe this has all grown out of my realization that I do not have to be "average" in anything I undertake with purpose. —L.F.

Sometimes overcoming negative prophecies takes decades. Each of these successfully completed goals—goals that this woman set for herself and has mastered—will accelerate her realization of the excellence that lies in her, waiting to be called forth. She is shedding negativity one layer at a time. So can we all.

My father always had a dream that I would attend college and obtain a degree. When he died, I found a note card left in his closet that said, "I know you will never finish college." I was struggling through my second year of college at the time and we'd had many arguments about me wanting to drop out. I will never know if he really believed that or was using psychology on me. It made me so angry and hurt that I made sure that I finished. —S.K.

Was this person's father using reverse psychology on her? Many times loved ones will try that tactic when nothing else seems to be working. It is a dangerous technique, given the human being's tendency to take words so literally, yet in this case it worked.

I learned after my father's death that he had once made a bet with one of his racquetball buddies that I would not last in business two years. This revelation has both haunted and fueled me. Although I've now been in business nearly twenty years, I can't help but wonder what he was thinking. Did he know something I didn't know? Or was it his own fear and inadequacy speaking?

My dad would tell me how stupid I was as a child, and I remember struggling with school and feeling like I was inferior. Yet in my teenage years, when my dad was too busy for me, I "adopted" a replacement dad. He, in return, adopted me in the sense of the word that he showed high esteem, respect, and belief in me. He did all he could do to make it possible for me to finish high school at a boarding school. I wanted to make him proud of me. I've been a successful father and community leader now for thirty years. I believe God sent positive people to help me overcome the negative messages I heard as a child and to help me become the successful person I am today. —L.K.

This is another case of a doubting father affecting the life of a child, yet this resourceful boy found a replacement dad to believe in him.

One woman shared with me that the negative prophecy she received was subtle yet powerful. Her mother, the only girl in her family to graduate high school, wanted to become a nurse. Her father refused her the $50 required (circa 1938) to fulfill her dream. She married, and the marriage was not happy. The woman telling me the story says, "Mother was extremely jealous and envious of others. I loved her, but often did not like her. I had to consciously choose not to drink my mother's sorrowful cup of envy and jealousy. I did become a nurse. My marriage is stable, with a husband who supports and celebrates my successes. I am sorry my mother was unable to fulfill her dream, but I did not let that fact keep me from fulfilling mine."

My mother told me that because I was in a wheelchair due to polio, people were not going to come to me, so I had better prepare to go out and approach people first. I thought, "How can I do that since I don't have access to the outside world?" I depended on everyone to get me where I needed to go. Maybe if I could learn how to drive, I reasoned, I could give myself some independence. I had the doctor test me to see if

I was strong enough to drive. He said, "No way!" This became fuel for me! One year later, I bought my own van and was driving. What independence! One of the first times I drove alone, two people stopped me and told me about an organization for people with disabilities, and that I should come to a meeting. I went, and that was the birth of my volunteer life. I have been going out to meet the people ever since then, and was recently recognized by the mayor for my outstanding contributions to the city. —*Susie Haake*

Susie did not let a physical challenge nor the opinion of a medical expert keep her from fulfilling her vision of having a life filled with contribution and others.

When I was in high school, I worked part-time for a neighbor who was a "gentleman farmer." He told me, "I like your work and attitude, and I want to give you a direct congressional appointment to the Naval Academy." No one had bestowed such a gift on me, and in my excitement I talked with my high school principal about this opportunity. I wasn't sure of my capabilities and wanted his support. He was a former naval officer, and he said to me, "You will never make it. You don't have what it takes." I was devastated, as I respected this man and wanted his encouragement.

Consequently, I turned down the appointment. Years later, though, after serving as an enlisted man, I completed my bachelor's and then my master's degree. My motivation was to prove him wrong. But, it took me several years before I felt worthy of seeking accomplishments and completing my degree. —*"William"*

This is one of the saddest and thus most meaningful examples of the impact people's prophecies have on us.

William was faced with two predictions:

(1) You can become a Congressional appointee to the Naval Academy, and
(2) You'll never make it.

One wonders if the high school principal's prediction carried more weight because he had more access to the young man. William took the negative prediction as truth, and thus charted his course on a lower, more traveled road. God wills for us only the highest and best, and was using the neighbor farmer as his prophet. But, William did not believe him, and thus never entered what might have been his "promised land."

My first grade teacher told my mother that I would probably never amount to much, because I did not apply myself. Eventually, I learned of this statement and came to resent and resemble it. I never enjoyed school as a child. I did mediocre at best. Upon graduation from high school, I was enrolled in a state college, but really had no desire to go. I dropped out after just three semesters, came home, and began to work. Fortunately, I went to work for a large company that provided tuition reimbursement for their employees. Finally, I decided the only way to get ahead at work was to complete my degree. I went back to school at night and on the weekends, and finished my degree in Management and Human Resources—magna cum laude. When I was able to walk across the stage with my honor cords on my graduation gown, it was like I had been able to deny the first grade prophecy and prove that I was *completely able* to apply myself *and* that I was intelligent! —*K.J.*

I am constantly amazed at how many people still carry predictions made about them as children throughout their adult lives. Here is a woman remembering a prophecy from her first grade teacher, even as she is walking across a stage, receiving a degree with honors. This only underscores the impact words have on children. They often become constant traveling companions for the child, for good or for ill.

Upon hearing of my decision to become a lawyer, my mother remarked that she thought I would be successful most of my life, but at the end of my career, I would probably have trouble being "the very best." True to her prediction, I have been a perennial runner-up, often a vice president, never a president. Her prediction affected my ability to finish. My expectation has always been to be second best, and I am still living that out. —C.G.

I can't imagine why any parent would put this image into a child's mind. Obviously, it is one that has haunted him all his life.

One therapist who works with women with breast cancer has them create a story about an imaginary woman who gets diagnosed with the disease. They are asked to write about how this imaginary woman successfully copes with the challenges of the illness and treatment. Having people write a new story with a happy ending for themselves is tremendously effective.

You, too, can write a new ending for your story, as these people did.

"Honey, now that we've got a little savings, let's buy a rental house and fix it up and then sell it." "Howard, if we do that, we could lose everything," said Edna. "Better to just stay with what we have." Ten years went by. "Edna, I saw a farm for sale down the road. We could buy a combine and then the boys could help us and we could start farming." "Howard, if we do that, we could lose everything," she said, not even looking up from her sewing. "Better to just stay where we are." The boys were doing their homework in the other room, but Charlie, the youngest, heard everything. He would always remember that sad, faraway look in his father's eyes, and the words his mother spoke as if they were the family litany.

So here he was, fifty-five years old, standing in one of my Path Training seminars. We were going through the exercises about the power of parents' unlived lives, and had now moved on to the subject of prophecy, where I asked each person to share what words had been prophesied over them.

I had first met Charlie the year before when I was speaking in Dallas. He was a successful real estate broker at the time, working on a book about motivation. Well dressed and smiling, he seemed on top of the world. It was with a great deal of delight that I welcomed him and introduced him at the seminar. Yet I was shocked when he stood up to share. No longer a real estate agent, he was now driving a limousine for a living. Recently divorced, he had also just filed bankruptcy. Somehow he had managed to make it to San Diego, and said that this weekend of reviewing his Path was exactly what he needed.

As I looked into his eyes, there seemed to be a calmness that surprised me. There was almost a sense of excitement lingering underneath his steady gaze. When he stood up to tell his story, it hit me. I said, "Congratulations, Charlie. You have managed with great finesse to live out both your parents' prophecies. What a talent you are!"

There was a shocked silence in the group. His eyes widened and he tilted his head. "I don't understand what you're saying. The world would label me a failure right now. I have lost everything."

"Exactly! You went out on a limb with your business and lost everything, just as your mother prophesied. At the same time, you have managed to free yourself from all your former entanglements, which is exactly what your father dreamed of doing. You have managed in one fell swoop to fulfill your debt to both your parents by making each of them right. Don't you see how brilliant that is? Now you can create the life *you* want, without the familiar sad and negative prophecies hanging over your head." Charlie turned negative prophecies into positive ones by walking through them.

Rachel Naomi Yemen is a physician who has chosen to work with critically ill patients—some of whom are in the final stages of their disease. In one poignant story from *Kitchen Table Wisdom* she recalls a young man referred to her who had been diagnosed with incurable liver cancer. A daredevil bon vivant, he had a history of injuries caused by hang gliding, race car driving, downhill skiing, and motorboat racing. Looking at his chart, Rachel immediately wondered if he hadn't had a death wish all along.

When she began to listen to the man talk, he shared about being the second, sickly son of a farmer and his wife in Iowa. His older brother was the picture of health, and was obviously his father's favorite. John, however, had been plagued with hepatitis and ear infections. When he was little he overheard his father declare in anger, "The truth is, Martha, if that boy were a pup I'd drown him." When John shared this story with Rachel there was no rage, no tears.

He got up and left the session, leaving Rachel to ponder his story. When he returned the following week she looked at him and said, "So, John—who are you going to side with, your mother who wants you to live, or your father who wants you to die?" There was a long silence. John finally burst into sobs at the stinging truth of her words. Finally, he stammered, "I want to live." She leaned forward and touched his knee and said, "I want you to live, too."

Silence filled the rest of the session. When John got up to go he looked at her, turned his head and smiled. "Finally, that jerk was outvoted once and for all."

Prophecy is a vote for life. And sometimes outcomes are determined by a single vote—by a single voice that says, "I don't care what others say. I want to live."

My friend Astrid said the call came late at night. Rachel, a sympathetic worker at Animal Control, said, "We have a dog in here that was picked up on an animal neglect charge. His ribs are sticking out through his skin, and tests show that he has heartworm. Everybody wants to put him down, but I know how you love boxers, and I thought maybe you'd want to see him before we do it." Astrid rushed down there the next morning, and said, "Yes, I'll take him." She brought him to PetSmart the next day so he could be with her while she worked at the adoption center. I came in to see him, and gasped while tears sprang to my eyes. This poor animal could not even hold up his head. His ribs and his hip bones had worn through the skin, so one could literally see the raw bone protruding from flesh. Raw sores covered most of his body. People walking by would drop to their knees in tears or start cursing the man who had done this to the dog, and angrily walk away.

"Even my volunteers say that I should put him to sleep. The vet bills are going to be about $700, and we have so many other dogs that need homes. But Laurie, I figured that he had made it this long, so he must really want to live. I'm going to name him Angel." I nodded that I understood, and gave her some money to help for his care, as did others who saw him. But I left thinking that he was not going to make it. "At least he'll die in loving arms," I thought.

Travels kept me from visiting her for several months. When I next visited the adoption center, I was greeted by a beautiful young tawny animal with a white blaze on his forehead and smiling eyes. "Wow, Astrid, this boxer's a beauty! Where did you find him?" "Laurie," Astrid smiled. "This is Angel." I didn't believe until I saw just the tiniest hint of where the skin had grown back over the hip bones and the ribs. "How did you do it?" "Science Diet, caring vets, and lots of love," she said. Several people came by while we were talking and asked if he was available for adoption. "No, not this one." She smiled. "He's my Angel." She knelt down and whispered, "You did want to live, my darling, didn't you." Angel licked her face, and then lifted his paw as if to say, "Yes, I did." Astrid turned a negative prophecy into a positive one.

Every day you and I walk down to the end of a pier. Two rowboats await us. One is made up of everything negative anyone has ever said about us. The other is made up of everything positive we have ever believed. Our job is to get to the other side of the lake. Which boat do we get into? The choice is ours alone.

Overcoming Negative Prophecies

We live in a world filled with negativity. There are so many broken and bitter people that few of us can escape having someone "curse us" in one way or another. Therefore it is important to be able to recognize a negative prophecy when you hear one, and be able to act or react accordingly.

Here are some steps which I have found helpful in overcoming negative prophecies.

1. ***Consider its source***. Is the person delivering it a reliable, proven source of information and wisdom in your life? Why should you trust them to know the future? Have they demonstrated success or knowledge in the area under determination?

   This is a hard one, because often recognized authorites can be wrong. As in the stories we just read, sometimes the source of the negative prophecy was a parent or a teacher or a principal or a counselor. An undiscerning person might consider them the end-all of information, yet, as was demonstrated, their information proved to be false.

   Fred Smith, the man who created FedEx, first came up with the idea for an overnight delivery service when he was a college student. He excitedly drafted his plan, showing how time and cost efficiencies could be saved by routing all the mail through one central hub. He got a "C−" on his paper. Yet

Fred Smith went on to establish his dream. Perhaps he might have thought to himself, "What does a college professor know about starting a business—especially one that has never been done before?" People who know business tend to be in business. Fred considered the source.

2. **Determine their motivation.** What do they have to gain if you fail? What would your success do to their identity and power base? One king in the Old Testament had four hundred prophets who were on his payroll. He was about to go into battle, and they all unanimously agreed that he was going to win. He smelled a skunk, however, and sent for the prophet he knew would tell him the truth. (*1 Kings 22:5–12*) Is this negative prophet on your—or on someone else's—payroll? Do they have an ax to grind with you? Would they just love to see you fail?

I will never forget my ex-husband shouting at me as I drove off: "God will not honor your ministry! You are going to fail!" This "curse" of course had more to do with his ego than with any direct connection he had to God. Thankfully, God has honored my ministry, despite a jealous man's negative prophecy. Nehemiah was able to discern that a messenger who came to him claiming he had a message from God was not sent by God, but by an enemy trying to thwart his progress. "Then I perceived that God had not sent him at all, but that he pronounced this prophecy against me because Tobiah and Sanballat had hired him. For this reason he was hired, that I should be afraid and sin, so that they might have cause for an evil report." *(Nehemiah 6: 12–13 King James Version)*

3. **Look for the truth in it.** Sometimes our enemies can be our best friends, if they point out weaknesses that others who love

us are willing to overlook. Clare Booth Luce is reported to once have said: "I miss my enemies terribly, for they helped define me."

Perhaps this "critic" is seeing a pattern in you or a trend in your behavior which, if left unchecked, might lead to your destruction. Certainly in some of the stories that we have read the critics had seen, or were seeing, trends in behavior that might have proven true, if the person in question had not taken a different action.

4. *Change your ways*. Proverbs 4:26 reads "Ponder the path of your feet." Psalms also says "I looked at the direction of my feet, and changed my ways." *(Psalm 119:59)* Ask yourself: "If I don't change what I am doing on a day to day basis, where will I most likely end up?"

Jonah's message to Nineveh was a serious one, and Nineveh listened. His negative prophecy did not come true because they repented, and changed their ways.

5. *Use the negative prophecy for fuel*. Many people are actually empowered by the negative predictions of others. If there is no truth in the negative words, or you don't intend for there to be truth in them, say to them, "Thank you for the fuel you just gave me!" and use it to spur yourself on.

6. (*Be persistent*). People who are prophets do not let circumstances interfere with their vision of the future.

John Sherrill, roving editor for *Guideposts* magazine, gives a hilarious account of persistence in his essay "Outsmarted." (*Guideposts* 2/99) He says that he was determined not to let a squirrel rob the birds of their seeds. When he noticed the squirrel had climbed the pole to the bird house, he built it higher. The squirrel just climbed higher. "I greased the pole. This merely added five seconds to his ascent. I punctured an empty plastic milk bottle and slid it halfway up. He used it as a stepping stone. I bought a section of stovepipe and suspended it around the pole. He squeezed through it. I filled the pipe with crushed plastic bottles. He bit into the plastic and dragged the bottles out. I bought a c-clamp and screwed it across the bottom of the stovepipe to hold the bottles in. This seemed to do it. The squirrel couldn't make it around the baffles." Yet the next day, John says, there the squirrel was again, munching on the sunflower seeds. He set up watch to see how this engineering feat was accomplished.

He saw the squirrel take a running start, leap, hit the stovepipe, career off it, sail, twist in mid-air and grab the feeder with split second timing. At this point John surrendered and now puts out extra sunflower seeds for the squirrel. This squirrel's persistence was his own prophecy. "I will get those sunflower seeds. I will . . ." This squirrel overcame all of John's negative prophecies.

7. **Take the time to examine your past**. If you do not understand where you came from, you might likely trip up and slide back there.

Let's face it, whether we like it or not, the past formed a comfort zone for us which we must consciously leave—often with great effort. Remember, it takes ten million gallons of fuel to launch a space craft beyond the pull of gravity. Your past represents your gravity. Are you willing to expend the energy it takes to move beyond it?

8. **Be aware of your surroundings**. A woman who realized that her whole atmosphere at home was one of negativity said

it simply and best when she said, "So I got out of there."

Sometimes you must put physical distance between you and an atmosphere that is sucking you in. If the negativity is from an isolated source, perhaps you can wrestle with it successfully and win. If it is coming at you from multiple sources, however, be willing to "get out of there," lest you, too, become subject to its negative pull. We are exhorted in Proverbs 4:27 to "Remove your feet from evil."

9. **Never quit.** As reported in the book *Changing for Good,* Dr. James Prochaska at the University of Rhode Island surveyed 30,000 subjects who were trying to make a change in their lives. Of those 30,000, those who tried and failed to change within a thirty-day period were twice as likely to succeed as those who didn't try at all. Of the two hundred subjects who made New Year's resolutions and were still keeping them two years later, nearly all of them averaged *fourteen* lapses before reaching a successful maintenance stage. Are you going to just quit after one failure?

10. **Claim God's miraculous saving power.** "If any person is in Christ, he or she is a new creation. Behold, all things have passed away, and all things are become new." *(2 Corinthians 5: 17 King James Version)* Believe God's prophecies about you.

11. **Determine never to issue words which could discourage or hinder someone's progress.** Don't leave any tangled up fishing wire on the river bank that might snare or entrap others. Let the words of your mouth always be discerning, encouraging and true.

12. **Forgive.** The quickest way to cut loose from someone else's fishing wire is to forgive them for leaving it—even if they

planted it there. Recognize that God allowed them to be a part of your story, if only for dramatic value. As Joseph said to the brothers who had sold him into slavery, "It was not you who sent me here, but God." *(Genesis 45:8 King James Version)*

Remember, in Christ we are guaranteed a happy ending. Don't enslave others with your anger. (It is not only unnecessary and counterproductive, it also adds wrinkles.)

Questions:

1. What negative prophecies were given to you growing up?

_____

_____

2. Who gave them to you?

_____

_____

3. What was your reaction?

_____

_____

4. How have these prophecies shaped your life:
   in a negative way?

_____

   in a positive way?

_____

_____

5. List all negative prophecies you have received indirectly through society, the media, and your culture. Determine to prove them wrong.

_____

_____

Meditation

Dear Lord,
Nearly all of us encounter false prophets on our spiritual journey.
You yourself predicted this, and warned against it. Help me
discern when someone's words are not coming from you. Help me
remember that your desire is always toward good, not evil. Help
me see any truths in the negative words of others which might be
pointing me to an outcome that could happen, if I do not change
my ways. Help me take the necessary steps to ensure that all
negative prophecies spoken against me become fuel that I use to
bring me closer to you, and a positive future.
  Amen.

Section II
Sources of Prophecy

Learning to Recognize the Messengers

The Prophecy of Family

The Prophecy of Friends and Strangers

The Prophecy of Professionals

The Prophecy of Angels

The Prophecy of Animals

The Prophecy of Scripture

The Prophecy of Dreams and Visions

The Prophecy of Family

"And it seemed to me that there were human
hands underneath its wings."

Ezekiel 10:11

In looking at the concept of family as messengers of prophecy, I noticed that parents prophesy to their children in several ways. The first is by example. The second is by creating an environment of expectations. The third is through direct verbal communication. The fourth is by the names and nicknames they call their children, or allow them to be called. The list is simple, yet profound.

Every word, task, or action that a parent takes toward a child is like pruning and shaping a bonsai tree. Trim off this branch, the tree will take one shape. Leave it, and it will take another. And in some families the rituals they practice and allow create subconscious patterns of behavior for children.

Six-year-old Joseph was eating dinner at the table with his mother, father, and four-year-old brother, Jacob. Jacob was clowning around, chewing his food with his mouth open and then opening it wider to display its half-chewed contents. His mother, in mock horror, asked, "Jacob, how are you ever going to get a girl to go out with you if that is the way you act at the dinner table?" Joseph replied, "That's easy. Just tell her it's a family tradition." Even a six-year-old was catching on to patterns that can be claimed by families as a justification for unusual behavior.

A friend of mine comes from an Italian family, where the way they show affection is to serve pasta and then yell at one another. When she entered the business world, she had to watch herself at Italian restaurants, because her first inclination was to lovingly insult her clients. It was her family tradition.

Another friend of mine married into an Irish clan that loves to party. When she confronted her teenage sons about her concerns over their developing drinking habits, they put their arms around her and said laughingly, "But Mom, we're Irish. This is the way we are supposed to act."

In his political tell-all *Just in Time*, George Stephanopolous talks about the family influence and expectations he grew up with, being a son whose father was a minister, as were his grandfather and uncle. No matter what the Greeks in his neighborhood did, George observed that "In my family, ethnicity overruled ideology." Some things were never to be questioned.

One of the most telling examples of family expectations is told in the story of Jacob and Esau. The Israelites were known for passing blessings on to their eldest sons—blessings which were so sacred and honored that they were considered prophecies. Jacob learned early that being second born meant that he would basically get zilch, even though as a fraternal twin he missed the first place slot by a matter of mere seconds. As you may recall in the story, Jacob was the favorite of his mother Rebecca, who hatched the plot to trick Isaac into giving the positive prophecy to Jacob, not Esau.

The first giveaway came when Esau, a hunter who loved Jacob's "potash stew," came in starving from the field. Jacob withheld it from him, saying he would only give it to him if Esau sold him his birthright. "What good is a birthright to a man about to die of starvation?" Esau bellowed, and made the deal that ultimately cost him his fortune. As one fourth grade student recalled in a Sunday School essay, "and that is how Jacob tricked Seesaw out of his copyright."

The confirmation of this came when Isaac, so old he could no longer see, was about to confer his final blessing on Esau. Rebecca tied goathide on Jacob's arms, rubbed dirt all over him, and had him take his father his famous stew. "Esau, is that you?" Isaac asked. In the first of what would be many lies, Jacob said, "Yes, Father, it is I." Isaac asked again, "Is that really you?" And once again Jacob replied in the affirmative. The ruse worked, and Jacob tremblingly received the positive prophecy of his father.

"May God give you dew from heaven, the richness of the earth, abundance of grain and wine. Let peoples serve you and nations bow low before you! Be master of your brothers, let your mother's other sons bow low before you. Accursed be whoever curses you, and blessed be whoever blesses you." —*Genesis 27:28-29*

Note that Isaac's prophecy was bold, and fairly specific. He didn't just say, "You will go on to do great things."

True prophecies, good prophecies, are not just well meaning generalized statements. Parents, in order to give valid prophecies, should go the extra mile to make it specific.

I am reminded of a story my mother just told me. She came down with that horrible flu virus that knocked so many of us out one winter. As any of you recall who had it, it sapped the energy right out of you for weeks. One of her well-meaning neighbors called and said, "Irene, I heard you were sick, so I'm sending over some chicken soup." Mom, who was so weak she could barely stand, was delighted, and as she pressed the phone to her congested head she heard the neighbor say, "And you can keep the pan when you're done." So Mom heard the knock on the door and dragged herself out of bed to open it. There, sitting on her newspaper on the front porch, was an uncooked, unopened can of chicken soup. Mom dutifully picked it up, disappointed that she had to open the can and cook it herself. She had been expecting a warm, steaming bowl of homemade soup. "I know now that what she said was 'And you can keep the can,' " Mom laughed. Still, it was a lesson for me.

Many of us just release well meaning sentences like "You're going to do great." "You are a terrific kid." "I am so proud of you." "You're going to go far." These are all positive statements—just like that can of soup was a positive gift. But how much more would it mean if the can had been opened, cooked, and stirred a little bit? A good prophecy is like soup that has been opened, cooked, and stirred . . . one in which you can identify the ingredients . . . and savor the healing odor even as you feel its warmth sink into your bones.

One thing parents help establish in their children is the prophecy of perspective. Parents are constantly setting up information filters for their children by how they view the world. Like the story I shared in *Jesus in Blue Jeans* about Irene teaching Jacob that change is fun and good by laughing with him when his balloon popped suddenly, parents teach children how to interpret events, and that mindset often becomes a prophetic compass.

In the Academy Award–winning movie *Life Is Beautiful*, a father who is thrown into a concentration camp by the Nazis, along with his six-year-old son and wife, turns the experience into a game in order to help his son cope. "Whoever wins 1,000 points gets to drive out of here in a real tank!'' he exclaims to the wide-eyed child. "These real mean men are trying to make us afraid, because anyone who cries gets points taken away from them. Anyone who asks for a snack or a jelly sandwich gets points taken away from them. But anyone who learns how to hide under the bunks and doesn't peek, no matter what, gets 60 points!'' With this ongoing fantasy he was able to keep the child enthralled and intrigued in one of the worst disasters imaginable. Indeed, the war ended and the little boy got to ride out of the concentration camp in an Allied tank, just as his father had prophesied.

His father's totally positive perspective became a prophecy that pulled the child into a happy ending.

A family setting can often become a mold—with negative consequences.

A friend of mine went to visit her sister-in-law in the hospital, and was amazed to note that the mother who was sitting by her daughter's side had bandages on her wrist and ankle exactly where the daughter had them. All the medical experts could not find anything clinically wrong with the sister-in-law, yet perhaps her "dis-ease" with the world came from the mother sitting beside her.

Unless parents make a conscious effort to change their lifestyle, odds are that their children will gravitate toward the patterns and lifestyle which is familiar, and duplicate it. Statistics show, for example, that women who saw their mothers getting beaten or mistreated by their spouse will tend to marry abusive men, regardless of their professional status. Sons who see their fathers hunched over the bills with a worried look on their faces will tend to view money as a precious and scarce commodity.

These are the unconscious prophecies broadcast twenty-four hours a day that often determine a child's picture of the future.

There is a scripture which reads "The fathers have eaten sour grapes, and the children's teeth are set on edge."(*Ezekiel 18:2 King James Version*)

Parents have a tremendous responsibility to not let their past hurts and disappointments become the prophetic limitations of their children. Joe Kennedy, Sr. declared to his second son, John, "Your brother Joe, Jr. would have made a terrific president. Now that he's dead, you will have to do."

When our parents speak, we tend to believe them. And, ever after, our activities are attempts to gain their blessing.

A word from a parent, or even a look, can be eternally recorded in a child's mind as a guideline for the future. A grandmother or grandfather, an aunt, can say a simple sentence that will become the most powerful guiding force in a child's life.

The simple stories which follow remind us that many of us can remember a defining moment when we received "a prophecy" from within our family, and how those simple words not only helped us determine our worth, but also set us on a course of action.

Parents

For example, did this mother merely observe, or actually shape her children's future with her words?

Mother called each of us by phrases, like "you're the smart one," "you're the pretty one," "you're my athlete," and "you're a hard worker."

I was "the smart one." I always took school very seriously, carried honor roll grades (this was expected of me, but not of my siblings) and went to college. To this day I strive to excel and keep on top of my career.

My sister was "the pretty one." Today she will not leave home without makeup on, every hair in place, and is constantly discussing her weight and appearance.

My oldest brother was "the hard worker." He started working as a farmhand at age eleven and co-owns a business with my mother.

My younger brother was "the athlete." He played football and baseball in high school. He now has two boys and he coaches Little League, and is an active member of the Pee Wee Association in his village. Sports are a major focus in his life. —T.H.

Here is a brief but beautiful example of a deathbed prophecy that gave a young girl faith in herself, and a certain awareness of a gift her father saw in her.

When my father was dying from cancer, he called me to his bedside and gave me a prophecy. He said, "You are a fruitful vine, and you will always display the fruits of the spirit." He began to name them one by one and as I rushed to get a pencil and pad he said, "I know you will remember them, because you have a good memory." I never knew he saw that in me. To this day, however, people comment on how sharp my mind

is, and are amazed at how I am able to recall events and items
and names.

I believe that this is because my father added an eighth fruit
to the vine of the Spirit: love, joy, peace, patience, gentleness,
kindness, goodness, self-control, meekness, *and* "a good
memory." —*E.D.*

A mother in this next anecdote told this child that she would
someday "be someone's boss." Notice that she did not call her
"bossy," which the child might have been. Rather, the mother
took a characteristic she saw in her child and turned it into a
positive prophecy.

As a child, my mother constantly asserted that I would one
day be "someone's boss"! Although I've never given much
thought to her prophecy prior to now, I now am revisiting the
question as to how I arrived at the point of becoming a manager supervising the activities of twenty-six people. —*C.S.*

In the following story, this woman's mother prophesied a
positive future for her daughter despite her having a physical
handicap.

I have an inherited eye disorder, which was diagnosed when I
was in high school. My mother also had this same condition.
She was a registered nurse, but could not see to work anymore.

She prophesied that nothing (certainly not an eye condition) would keep me from college, a career, my own children,
or anything else I determined that I wanted. If I felt down or
wanted to feel up, she would empathize with me for a few

minutes, but then would kick me out the door to be on my way . . . doing whatever it was that I thought I couldn't do. Skiing, horseback riding, going to school, working and parenthood all followed. I am now an occupational therapist and direct a rehab department of more than 50 people. Mom's been gone five years . . . I do miss her *kick.* —J.B.

Often, a parent's role becomes very much like the parent Jesus spoke about in the story about the prodigal son. Despite our best efforts and intentions, sometimes children go astray. As a parent then our work becomes perhaps the hardest—keeping the vision of them as whole and happy in our mind, until they return to us as we stand waiting and watching for them at the gate.

I was a heroin addict for over fifteen years and spent several years in prison. People would tell me I was never going to be anything, that I was going to die in prison. They said I was going to use heroin for the rest of my life.

But my mother would constantly tell me, "I know that someday God will change your life, and someday you'll work for Him." I now work with a teenage counseling organization and I visit people in jails, preach God's word, and share a love that I never knew before. Thank God, Mom was right. —*Anonymous*

When I was young I was a real troublemaker—always fighting other boys and breaking others' things. Once my dad told me when I was real mad that I would make him proud someday, and have a family of my own to love. My dad watched me get worse with each passing year, but he never gave up on me. I

went to prison for armed robbery. I was arrested for man-
slaughter, but was later released for justifiable homicide. Eventually I did a few years in prison for my crimes. One day I hit
rock bottom and was real tired of wasting life, so I went
straight. I have four children, a loving wife and I've been out
of trouble for thirteen years now. With God's help I have fulfilled my dad's prophecy. —*Anonymous*

Involving children in our activities becomes a very powerful
prophecy for them. The stories that follow show how a parent's
confidence and expectations for a child are often conveyed as
much in deeds as in words.

In the early fifties, when I was a teenager, my father basically
said that I could be anything I wanted to be. I don't remember
him saying it aloud, but he would show me this through his
actions and respect. If he needed help working on a car, he
would call me. He even let me have a car in high school back
when girls didn't do that. But I did have to know how to take
care of it. I didn't really realize that women were discriminated
against. No one ever told me that, especially my father, so I
have never accepted it. —*D.S.*

A father who needed help working on a car and called his
daughter over to help him fix it taught a thousand sermons to
her, just as the father who gave his daughter a typewriter when
she was a child.

I grew up in a home that was supportive of education and hard
work. My father always told me that I could do whatever I set

my mind to. At an early age, he discovered I enjoyed the office environment and noticed me playing on my grandfather's old Corona typewriter, vintage 1900.

He encouraged me by buying a new typewriter, and a "teach yourself" course when I was eight years old. He hinted that I share my interest with a new close friend of the family, who happened to be the school secretary at my elementary school. She encouraged me and was my role model. I became a Professional Legal Secretary at the age of 21.

I am proud of all I have become, and I hope my father is, too. Thank you. —G.H.

Guideposts magazine recently carried an article about an insightful young mother. Knowing that she would be missing out on some of her children's most meaningful moments, she came up with a creative way to be a positive prophet and presence in their lives, even when she was gone.

Nan was a nurse on a chemotherapy unit, and was assigned to care for Rebekah, the thirty-two-year-old mother of three little girls who was undergoing treatment for breast cancer. As the weeks went by, Rebekah's condition worsened, and she asked Nan if she would be kind enough to bring her a tape recorder and some blank tapes. Nan did, bringing them to Rebekah the next day. When Rebekah's husband and little girls left after visiting hours were over, Rebekah took out the tape recorder and a notebook. As Nan was leaving she heard Rebekah begin "Molly, this is for you on your fifth birthday . . ." Rebekah eventually recorded sixty tapes for the little girls, anticipating birthdays, graduation, prom dates, and even their wedding days. Rebekah died shortly after making the last tape, but she had left behind a legacy as a parent that would live on. She left them a whole lifetime of positive prophecies.

Children are very aware of the prayers and prophecies prayed over them.

My mother told me that when I was a child, she presented me before God in the temple, praying and predicting that I would become a priest. She did this while still in the Catholic church, and she did it with the rest of my brothers and sisters as well. Eventually, our family switched denominations, yet her prophecies evidently transferred with the family to the new church setting. Of the twelve children she had, seven of us became full-time ministers, including me. —*J.H.*

A Brother

Often other members of the family can be the ones who speak prophetic words to us.

My mother recently returned from Provence, France. She brought back with her a book about Vincent Van Gogh, the world renowned artist, who had lived and painted there. As I eagerly read and absorbed each page of the book, I was surprised to learn that Vincent had originally begun his professional career not as an artist but as a pastor. His enthusiasm for life, and his desire to help the poor people all around him, caused him to constantly give away his possessions.

His brother Theo noticed that Vincent had a gift for painting, and encouraged him to make that his vocation, offering to pay him out of his own wages to help support the endeavor. So Vincent began to paint the lives he saw around him—people huddled around a table by firelight, eating the potatoes they had gotten that day from the fields. He painted purple irises in a vase, and the way the stars looked at night, pointed to by the cypress trees that were planted throughout the landscape to help cut the effects of the mistral winds. He painted a reaper working in a glistening field of wheat, writing in a letter that the reaper reminded him of death, working away among the sheaves in broad daylight, without malice or foreboding.

Yet Vincent's paintings were met with scorn. The villagers and critics mocked him, using his paintings for target practice or to hang on their hen house doors to keep the wolves away. Theo constantly encouraged Vincent anyway, telling him not to give up his God-given talent. Vincent painted furiously for five or six years, turning out more than two thousand paintings. During that time he sold only two—just enough for food and supplies.

The correspondence between Vincent and his brother totaled more than six hundred letters. Vincent, affected by seizures and bouts of despair, committed himself to a local asylum, seeking peace from the crushing depression that haunted him. Perhaps today he would have been helped with chemical balancing drugs and therapy. At that time, there were no such interventions, and Vincent ended up killing himself one "starry, starry night." Penniless, and insane.

Vincent died at the age of thirty-seven, and Theo, his brother, who was just a few years older, died six months later—also a poor man.

Today, Vincent Van Gogh's work is among the highest priced and most sought after in the world. The purple irises in a vase that he painted one afternoon alone in his room sold at auction for forty-two million dollars.

"Theo" comes from a Latin combining form meaning God. Vincent Van Gogh's prophet was his brother.

Children

Sometimes it may be our children who encourage us, or help set us on a path. In her wonderful new book, *It's Only Too Late If You Don't Start Now*, Barbara Sher shares the prophecy of encouragement given to her by her young son. As a struggling single mother who felt a call to write but could not seem to find the time to do so while running a business and raising young children, she came home one day to find that her son had taken a small stuffed moose from his room and attached it to the kitchen door. Next to it was a sign written in very large letters: WRITE OR WE KILL THE MOOSE.

Amy Biehl, an idealistic and beautiful young woman, had gone to South Africa with one desire—to help people in the country make a better life for themselves. Tragically, she was violently murdered while there. Her parents were stunned and saddened. Yet, when they went to retrieve her body, they came to a life-changing decision. They would both leave their jobs in America and come to South Africa to continue her work. They have helped build a school and a bakery which will better the lives of all the people in a small, out of the way village Amy gave her heart—and life—for.

Amy was a child prophet, whose words and deeds became a prophecy for her amazing parents.

Aunts and Uncles

As an aunt I take very seriously my role in my nieces' and nephews' lives, even though it may seem marginal compared to that of parents. The Broadway musical *Auntie Mame* tells the story of a boy whose wild and crazy aunt taught him the meaning of life, love, and happiness, while his parents were only interested in getting him out of their hair. I believe that my uncle Joe helped cultivate a love of words in our family, as he was constantly buying us games like Scrabble and Password. He loved nothing more than playing games with words, and the times he would come over and play with us are still cherished in my mind. He helped influence my desire to be a writer.

A Mother-in-law

Another family member who can bear a positive influence is that of the mother-in-law. Although jokes are often told about how unwanted and annoying mothers-in-law can be, in truth they can become "bonus" mothers who help shape our lives. Such was the case with Ruth, whose story of her journeys with Naomi are detailed in the Old Testament, and such is the case with Kevin, who shares his story here.

My mother-in-law gave me a positive prophecy when I was just out of college. I had bounced a few checks, and as a result the bank manager impatiently closed out my account. My mother-in-law walked in with me by her side, told the branch manager, in front of the entire bank, "*One day* you will regret

losing this man as a customer." She believed in me long before
I had accomplished anything and her words have propelled me
to go further in my life than anything else. I will never forget
that day. I became a very successful stockbroker, in charge of
millions of dollars of assets, and part of my driving force was
to prove my mother-in-law right. —K.B.

Husbands

The word husband is related to "husbandman," which means
gardener. Paul spoke about a man loving his wife the way Christ
loved the church, encouraging her and loving her enough even to
die for her. While traditionally women have been the encouragers
and nurturers, men are now beginning to recognize and take seriously their role as nurturers, as well. As the founder of Promise
Keepers shared in a television interview, "If you want to know if a
man is doing his job as a husband, look at his wife. Is she flourish-
ing? Is she glowing? Is she nurtured and supported in every way?"
This woman's husband has become a prophet for her, as well.

One fall my husband and I were talking about my desire to
become a building contractor. I wondered how other builders
got started and who they were and what they had that I didn't.
Two months later, my husband saw an ad in the paper for an
independent contractor position for a large builder. He encouraged me to take the job. To make a long story short, I
went to work for him and two months later I bought the company with two other male partners. We have built twenty cus-

tom made homes since we started. My husband has continued to be very encouraging and supportive. He's my very own cheerleader! —C.P.

Grandparents

Surveys have shown that the grandparent is often the most trusted of all family members, and thus can be the most influential. As one child told his grandfather, "A grandpa is like a father except with more time."

I remember my grandfather as a kind and generous man who always seemed to have a twinkle in his eye. He would look at me with so much love that it was almost palpable. He taught me how to collect rocks and sharpen knives and look for patterns in pieces of wood that always told a story. He was one of the finest men I ever met.

My mother felt the same way about her grandfather, Otto. Otto had evidently been quite a swashbuckling romantic in his time, as he helped my grandmother escape from an arranged marriage in Germany and hid her on a boat to America, where they were going to make their fortune. Grandpa "Otto" started a coffeehouse in New York, and he and his wife and Mom lived above it for many years. My mother's mother, Irene, was working two jobs and was so stressed out about the children that she actually put up two of Mom's half brothers for adoption. Mom's grandmother resented Mom being there, and would always tell her how much she was "costing them." But Mom remembers that after a long day at the shop Grandpa Otto would come home and take her in his arms and just laugh and hold her, telling her how pretty she was and that she was the light of his life.

Recently my sister found a tiny button photograph of Otto, and had it restored and enlarged to give to Mom as a birthday present. Kathy asked me to keep it, and when Mom walked into her room and saw the photograph she said, "That looks like my grandfather Otto." "It is," I smiled. Mom suddenly gasped and clutched her heart. Tears sprang to her eyes, and she couldn't talk for several minutes. After she finally calmed down I asked her to explain her reaction. Still choked up, she replied, "Grandpa Otto was the only person in my childhood who showed me unconditional love. In fact, I think he was the only man who ever truly loved me."

Another friend of mine has had a challenging and at times difficult relationship with her mother. Perhaps because they are so much alike, they refuse to show overt signs of affection. Yet Randi says it was her grandmother, Margara, who made her feel loved and special. She used to call her "Reyna," which means "Queen," and show her off to all her friends. She taught her literature and dance and told her that someday she would grow up to be a great ambassador. The day Margara died Randi said she wanted to climb into the grave with her. Randi felt her life was ending and that she would never again be loved the way Margara loved her.

The best thing grandparents provide is love. And sometimes they speak words for us which become prophecies.

My Grandma was a strong, independent woman with dreams of being a fashion designer, but she didn't have the wherewithal to work in that profession. I spent summers with her and drank in her spirit. By fifth grade, I began sewing all my clothes, and in high school, I worked in fabric stores creating things for customers.

I eventually went to design school and once sat in a lecture by a New York designer who said only 3 percent of all design students would end up in a design position. That was the challenge I needed. Now I am the vice president of design at a $20 million company, and I keep my grandmother's picture on my desk as a reminder of how, and maybe why, I'm here. —L.S.

When I was nine, I had been playing with my siblings and cousins at my grandparents' house, and we got into a typical childhood fight about who got to go first or who was best. I remember my grandmother taking me aside and complimenting me. She called me a "precious peacemaker."

This was probably far from an accurate description of my character, as the oldest of a string of five cousins, I'm sure I was quite a bossy little leader. But as she spoke those words, I remember immediately seeing my new job as being to keep the peace among the cousins whenever we were together.

Several times throughout my life, others have commented about my ability to bridge the gap between apparent opposing forces. What a gift she gave me! Her words helped shape how I see myself—and try to act, in every situation. —A.D.

Grandparents, like other family members, are important messengers and prophets who help shape the way we see ourselves, and the way we see ourselves helps determine our future.

Questions:

1. What was the family prophecy? If you didn't have one, what do you think it was? For example:

"We are the McCoys, and this is how the McCoy family handles money."

Now you fill in the blank.

"We are the _____, and this is how the _____ family handles _____."

2. Analyze how this prophecy may be affecting you and/or your children. For example, my family "mantra" was "Keeping up with the Joneses!" (Don't think this hasn't had a profound influence on me. I grew up thinking that we were the family that had to set the pace for everyone else.) What were your family's expectations?

_____

_____

3. What words did your parents use to describe you to others? To yourself?

_____

_____

4. What words do you use to describe your children—to others? To themselves?

_____

_____

5. What positive things have family members said to you which caused you to soar?

_____

_____

6. How can you make sure that people in your family, especially the children, are getting positive prophecies from you?

_____

_____

7. Sit down today and write a positive prophecy for everyone in your family—no matter what age they are. It could shape their future in ways you'll never know.

Meditation

Dear Lord,
You have given us all a positive prophecy by inviting us to join
your family. Help me study the prophecies you have given to your
disciples, and claim them as my own. Help me consciously pass on
positive prophecies to members of my family, seeing in them and
calling forth in them all that is good.
*   Amen*

The Prophecy of Friends
and Strangers

"There is one thing every human being needs—young or old, rich or poor, male or female, black or white—and that is a friend." So says Harv Oodstyk, founder of the Step Poverty Fighting Program in Dallas, Texas, and Washington, D.C. Harv is now sixty-five years old, tall, and handsome with a sculpted face fringed by shocking white hair. The people he works with—the people he loves—call him "Moses." For forty years he has been working in areas like Harlem and southwest Dallas, calling people out of poverty, substance abuse, and crime. His one and only weapon is to become their friend.

When he first started he played basketball with the youth, hanging out at the courts with a six-pack of sodas and a silly grin. If he beat them they'd have to take him to their leaders—who were most often tough kids already embarking on a life of crime. Harv would hang out with them and challenge them to look at a new way of being.

He helped one twelve-year-old get a new set of teeth so he could smile without hiding his face, or fighting the kids who teased him. He helped a young mother on welfare get a job and inspired a grandmother to go back to school—to get her GED, and her college degree. This woman, whom Harv calls "Ms. Maria," now has a goal of becoming an attorney. Harv smiles. "She'll do it, too." Ms. Maria stood with tears in her eyes and said,

"Harv, and Jan, and the rest of the team came and put their arms around me like a cloak. They helped me walk through the valley of my fears one step at a time—until here I am standing before you, a college graduate."

It is amazing what friends can do. No wonder Proverbs states that "the pleasantness of one's friends springs from their earnest counsel." (*Proverbs 27:9*) Two friends who have been prophets to me are Jan Sterrett and Catherine Calhoun.

Growing up the main prophecy I received was that "I could do anything I set my mind to." Like many children, I began gathering information about what I should set my mind to do, and was both drawn to and repelled by my father's demand for me to be number one at something. My mother only wanted us all to be creative and happy, and to work for a larger dream. Somehow I settled on advertising as my kingdom for success.

Yet God provided for me a prophet in the form of Jan Sterrett, the mother of one of my closest friends. Jan had given her daughter Linda a prophesy about me which was conveyed to me second hand. Linda and I were having lunch one day, and I jokingly scribbled a little poem on a napkin as we were waiting for our order to arrive. When we got up to leave Linda carefully gathered the napkin and put it into her purse. "Why are you doing that?" I asked her. "Because my mother told me to save every letter, every note, every scrap of paper you write on, even if it's directions on a napkin—because someday you are going to be a very famous writer." I threw my head back and laughed as we walked away. I was an eighteen-year-old lifeguard at the time. Yet mentally I put that pebble of a prophecy in my pocket, and it went with me wherever I went.

Twenty-two years later, as I was approaching my fortieth

birthday, that pebble caught fire and threatened to destroy everything I had built up—as far as my career—at that time. In fact,
it did destroy it, as I realized that I would never "become a great
writer" by writing advertising copy and television commercials.
That prophecy of Jan Sterrett's became for me like Moses' "burn-
ing bush." It called me to a new life adventure. As I detailed in
my second book, *The Path*, I then set out into the unknown to
see if her words could indeed become true.

After *Jesus, CEO* was published, Jan Sterrett flew down from
her home in Anchorage, Alaska to attend a book signing I was
doing in Seattle. She sat in the audience with tears streaming
down her face as I gave my talk. She then stood there beside me
as I was signing books, saying softly, "I knew this day would
come. I just knew it."

I often wonder where I would be today if Jan had not spoken
those words, and if Linda had not shared them with me. As Mom
jokingly said one day, "Honey, I have to admit I never saw it in
you. After all, I always beat you at Scrabble."

Another important role friends play is that of being mentors.
Advertisements on TV now urge people to become mentors. Programs like Big Brothers and Big Sisters have statistically proven
that kids who have mentors fight less, do better in school, and
tend to stay off drugs. Business publications claim that the quickest way to get to the top of your profession is to find a mentor.

This role in my life was undertaken by Catherine Calhoun.
When I was twenty-eight years old I was coming off a brilliant
and focused path as a divorced college drop-out/hostess/
babysitter/secretary/receptionist/kiddies' fun club director. To
say that I was on a career track would have been like saying a
rabbit was climbing the corporate ladder. Despite my promising

ascent in high school to the honors of valedictorian and "Most
Likely to Succeed," I had descended into a valley of pinball
knockaround—bouncing from one minimum wage job to another—dependent on whatever "The Lord would provide."
Fortunately, God provided Catherine.

All women I knew at the time were either teachers, secretaries, or nurses. None of those professions called me. My father,
who once used to recite proudly my high school accomplishments to his friends, had retreated to the point where he only
shared my racquetball scores. (To say he wanted me to succeed
even at that was an understatement. He used to get so nervous
before my racquetball tournaments that he would throw up the
night before.)

It was in this context that I got a job at the Women's Resource
Center, where I met Catherine. I watched her closely in her role
as Executive Director, which called for activities ranging from
writing grants, asking for donations, comforting battered wives,
and wrestling with Board members over budget issues. She did
all of this with a sense of humor, honor, and flair. Her carriage,
her confidence, her compassion, and her killer wardrobe were
like a promise from a far away land. I had met a woman who had
wings . . . a woman close to my own age who was showing me
what I might become. When she left the Resource Center to start
her own consulting company I watched her literally take to the
air—travelling five days a week, training people all over the country. Whether she knew it or not, she was helping me chart my
destiny.

Through our discussions about society's needs, to the role of
women, to the responsibility we each have to identify and live
our dreams, I heard a symphony that I could play in, too. The

fact that she took me with her to meetings and had me proof her grants or review slide by slide what she was teaching made me want to be a change agent, too. Because of Catherine, I knew it was possible.

Friends and mentors. Their love and belief in us becomes a prophecy. And much of what they communicate to us is in the form of role-modeling—of showing us in non-verbal ways how to be.

Gregory Jackson grew up as a poor black kid in the projects of southeast Dallas. Raised by his grandmother after his dad abandoned the family, Gregory nevertheless went on to get a college scholarship in football. After college many businesses tried to recruit him. But Gregory did what more of us need to do. He went back to his roots, and moved into the projects he once was so eager to leave. He went back to be a role model and mentor to kids like him.

He said, "I remember when I was growing up that the only men I saw hanging around the projects were shooting dice and drinking beer out of brown paper bags. So now that I have moved back I am always conscious to come home wearing a business suit, carrying a briefcase in one hand and a carton of milk in the other. I want those kids to see an image of the kind of man I never saw."

Friends and mentors help bring us focus, as well as unconditional support.

When people were asked, "What was the single most important intervention in you life?" ninety percent name a person. King David never would have made it to the kingship of Israel if Jonathan, his beloved friend, had not interceded for him on numerous occasions and actually helped him escape his father Saul's plans of destruction. Abraham saved his friend Lot's family from annihilation by praying for him and helping him escape a fiery death, and Moses acted as not only a prophet but as a friend when he prayed that God would spare the complaining and ungrateful Israelites. Elijah acted as a friend and mentor to Elisha, showing him the power of words. Mordecai helped steer Esther to her role in history through his faithful friendship and wise words of instruction. Mary Magdalene played the role of a prophet and friend by anointing Jesus' feet before burial, and Jesus reminded Peter of their deep friendship even after Peter had betrayed him three times. Paul acted as a friend and advisor to Timothy and Titus, helping them multiply their gifts. In fact, much of the New Testament consists of letters written to friends—filled with words which would shape individual lives, as well as change history.

Simple words of encouragement from these friends changed life directions for the people who heard them.

Mary was a petite junior high school student when I met her. As we became acquainted, she told me of her dream to be an airline pilot. She ended the story by saying it would never come true because she was a girl. I quickly told her that gender didn't matter to an airplane. It was exciting to see the possibilities begin to form in her mind.

Several months later, I ran into Mary. She excitedly began to tell me about her flying lessons and her first solo flight. A month or so later, she passed the tests for her license.

Today Mary is a flight instructor, building time and experience to get that job with the airlines. When she sees me, she always gives me the report of how many hours she has in the air and then with a grin, introduces me to her friends as the

guy who told her she could fly. Hearing that introduction sure
feels good! —J.W.

My father was an abusive alcoholic and my mother away from
home most of the time working two jobs. They both owned
and managed a tavern in our small town which basically kept
them either sleeping or working long hours. I am one of six
children. God sent us an angel in the form of our next-door
neighbor who was a retired nurse in her sixties. She started to
baby-sit me from the time I was a newborn. I became her "girl"
from that moment on. She always told me this story over and
over . . . with tears in her eyes every time . . . how one night
when I was a baby, and my parents came home, I clutched my
fist on her dress so tight that she would have had to break my
little hand if she had tried to release my grip. She looked at
me and said, "I hope you always cling like that to everything
I teach you." I have!

Because of her contributions, I was able to go on to college.
She died at age 87, my senior year at college. My father was
an atheist and my mother didn't know God, but this woman
was an angel, sent from God to save me and carry me through
an awful childhood. I am now a nurse, just like her! —T.H.

Sometimes, it is the words of a stranger which helps set us on
a new course.

I was a hairdresser in California in the 1980s. My shop was
across the street from the only high school in town. A cute
young man who was a regular customer was shocked one day

when he found out that I smoked cigarettes. He told me he thought I was a really terrific person and that smoking was beneath me. He was the first person who ever had verbally encouraged me to stop smoking. He told me he felt I could do anything. I finally did quit several years later and have never forgotten him. His encouragement is precious to me and has never lost its brightness, even after twenty years. —L.T.

As I travel around the country speaking I have found a niche in speaking to junior and senior high schools. Once, after I finished an assembly program in a very rural country school, a tall dark-headed student asked if we could talk. As he began to speak he started to cry uncontrollably, venting pain and built-up anger. After he calmed down, I talked with him about his goals, dreams and how to get there. When John left, I researched his background through some of his teachers. What was his story? I learned that John lived with his alcoholic dad and his sister in a trailer back in the hills. His home life was terrible and he had nothing to hold on to. A year later I was in the same county, but at a different school. As I was walking down the hall, I saw John, so I called to him. As he came up to me, his eyes were open wide, he was clean and well dressed. He looked at me and said, "How did you remember my name?" I said, "John, I will always remember you. You are my hero and a winner." As he shared, he told me his grades were up substantially, he was working toward graduation and even had a girlfriend. He explained, "The last time you came to the other school, you told me that you believed in me. That meant something to me. It made me think." The spoken word is powerful. —J.S.

Jackie DeFazio, President of the American Association of University Women, recalls in a letter to members how friends gathering together to help a common cause changed history.

The year was 1919. Europe had been ravaged by World War I. And radium was far too expensive for a scientist of modest means to afford for experiments. Even one as famous as Madame Marie Curie.

As a result, Madame Curie's ground-breaking research had reached a virtual standstill. That's when the American Association of University Women (AAUW) came to her rescue. AAUW members from Maine to California helped raise an astonishing $156,413 enabling Madame Curie to purchase one gram of radium and continue her experiments. These experiments that helped her create the field of nuclear chemistry and forever change the course of science. Madame Curie received the Nobel Prize for her work, helped along by a group of people who believed in her and showed it!

Most of the women who helped raise money for Madame Curie were unknown to her. Yet their actions and belief in her became a prophecy.

In 1979, I made a momentous decision. I left my job as a staff nurse and went to work in the ICU at a pediatric hospital. When I was interviewed, I was told by the manager that she would "take a chance" on me since I had no pediatric experience—if it didn't work out, she would fire me!

During my first week of orientation in the hospital, I was back in a supply room trying to figure out how to work an infant scale. I was feeling overwhelmed and frightened, and I felt I had made a terrible mistake in switching to the pediatric world. Suddenly, the door opened and a young nurse I had never seen walked in. She took one look at my face and asked, "What's wrong?" I blurted the whole story out to her, including my fears. To my surprise, she walked over, hugged me, told me that I was going to be all right, and that she knew I would do a great job in the ICU.

Somehow, I believed her. That day was a turning point in my life—I did indeed complete orientation and as my anxiety level decreased, I began to love working in the unit. A few years later, that nurse was transferred to the ICU where I became her preceptor. The young nurse and I became good friends and worked together for many years until she was tragically killed by a drunk driver. I write this to you as the director of nursing for both the intensive care unit and the transitional care unit of the same Children's Medical Center. After eighteen years of work, I guess they've decided to keep me.

This one thing I know—If God hadn't directed that young nurse into my path, I doubt I'd be here, loving what I am doing, and making a difference in lives of children, our most precious resource. I will never forget her gift, and I have tried to be the same type of empathetic cheerleader she was.

Everyone needs a positive push in the right direction from time to time and I'm so grateful that wonderful friend gave me mine. —E.T.

God so often speaks to us through strangers and friends.

Questions:

1. Which friends have given you prophecies which helped set the course of your life?

_____

_____

2. Has a stranger ever spoken to you words which proved to contain valuable messages in them?

_____

_____

3. When have you prophesied to a friend? Did it come true?

_____

_____

4. When can you prophesy to your friends? How?

_____

_____

5. Can you prophesy to people you barely know? How?

_____

_____

Meditation

Lord,

There is perhaps no truer calling than that of a friend. You say in Proverbs that "The wounds of a friend may prove faithful." Let me always and only speak strong words that heal and shape and inspire those around me.

Also, help me recognize that you may give me a word to speak that affects or encourages someone I barely know, and may never see again.

Help me be a faithful messenger to all I know—and meet.

Amen

The Prophecy of Professionals

I wonder how many of us realize the influence people outside the family can have on us—especially professionals who are entrusted to lead us and teach us in the way we should go.

Teachers

It was amazing to me how often people cite teachers as being the people they remember as uttering prophetic words. *Deuteronomy 32:2* reads, "Let my teachings fall like rain . . . like abundant rain on tender plants." And truly most of those who teach do so because their eyes are set on the future growth of their students.

Schools, which house and support our teachers, are indeed houses of prophecy.

I owe much of the success I've had in business to my teachers, two of whom I remember profoundly.

Mrs. Patricia Denham was my English teacher in grade school. She had a regal air about her that permeated the classroom. Kids who were screaming and chattering and knocking each other around in the halls suddenly became model students of behavior the moment they entered her classroom. Her only weapon of discipline was a raised left eyebrow. Mrs. Denham's emphasis was on penmanship as well as grammar. She opened up a world to me of poetry and literature and the ability to express my feelings about the words we read. I still cherish essays I wrote which had the words I most craved to see written across the top. "Well done." How I wanted to please Mrs. Denham with my thoughts and poems. In retrospect, her interest and approval of my work helped shape my destiny.

Pearl Crouch, my journalism teacher, was also a prophet to me. She had no pet students, rarely laughed, and had a phrase that we all came to dread. It was "You can do better than that." Yet she took a group of giggly teenagers and gave us a $50,000 budget to produce a high school yearbook and said, "This book is up to you. Now, let's go study the best." She scraped up enough money somehow to take a group of us to Dallas where we saw every award-winning college yearbook ever made and she took us on a tour of the production plant where the books were made and we came back wide-eyed with wonder and excitement and she saw to it the excitement never died. She taught me that a deadline is never to be missed and creativity means coloring outside the lines. Sometimes we would sit silently in her office and just hold books and feel their pages—caressing the textures of the paper and commenting on the weight of them in our hands.

Our yearbook that year won national awards and was the first designated "A+" book in the school's history. Ms. Crouch wrote in my yearbook a long letter the essence of which was: "To Laurie—a lover of books, and a seeker of spiritual truth. I pray that you never stop seeking." She died years ago of ovarian cancer. She did not recognize me by the time I was able to visit her, yet her belief in me was a prophecy.

*   *   *

Other people were also influenced by a teacher.

I was in the Air Force, uncertain about what I would do when my enlistment was up in two years. Since I had not been in school for a long time, I decided to take an evening course in my spare time.

I wrote a report and casually turned it in. To my surprise the instructor praised me in front of the class, saying, "You should be a teacher, rather than a student. You would do a great job." His words stuck with me, and I began to see a new career for myself.

After the Air Force, I enrolled in college full-time, got my degree in education, and then proceeded to teach college for the next twenty-four years. I am now very aware of how a teacher's praise might change the life of an uncertain student. —D.D.

When I was in first grade, I was failing. My schoolmates called me names like "hunk of junk," and even my teacher told me I was retarded. One day a substitute teacher came in class and defended me by telling the class that the twinkle she saw in my eyes told her that I was going to be a great man someday.

Today, I have a master's degree, was commissioned an officer in the U.S. Army, and now pastor a large congregation. I may not be great yet, but my best days are yet to come. —P.W.

One wonders what would have become of him had this substitute teacher not spoken into his life?

A long time ago, when I was finishing elementary school, my mother thought that my job for life should be to make dresses. (I didn't like that idea at all!) She looked for a school that taught dressmaking. One day when registration time came, my mother took me to that school and registered me, then we went to town to buy the school supplies. On the street we met my math teacher, who was a wonderful lady. When she learned what we were doing she said, "Wait a moment, your daughter has the potential to be a teacher. Go right now to the Teachers College and register her there." Reluctantly my mother did what she suggested. I studied for six years in that school and thoroughly enjoyed it. The work was hard, but I did it. I graduated as a teacher and happily taught for twenty-two years. —I.A.

This woman is grateful that a teacher intercepted a limiting family prophecy and replaced it with a new one tailored to her true talents and desires.

One place I found prophecy alive and well was in the churches. Because people there are in the business of rebuilding lives and encouraging one another, many influential and life-changing words can be spoken. The ministerial profession *should* be full of positive prophecy.

A music minister once told me, "God has found you trustworthy, and will place many lives into your hands." Today I am a teacher, adviser, and evangelist, who now leads people on their spiritual walk with God. I help them deal with their daily struggles, as well as with the condition of their hearts. Even though I started out as a gang member, destroying everything that I touched, God has literally placed hurting and thirsty souls into my hands. —*Anonymous*

Years ago a preacher at our church prophesied through prayer that God would use the gift of healing through me. I didn't really give it much thought until years later. A good friend of mine had a stroke and was in critical health. I went to visit him and he didn't recognize me. I sat down beside him and began to cry. All I could do was to begin praying for him. It was a simple prayer asking God to heal my friend. Then I said good-bye and left. As I walked away, I somehow knew that God would heal him.

The next day, he began to recover and within one week, he was back at home. That was twenty-three years ago and he is now eighty-nine years old and still going strong. —*B.K.*

People who participate in twelve step programs choose a sponsor to oversee their rehabilitation and provide ongoing support. In this case, a "sponsor" was also a prophet.

In 1985, I was preparing to reenter civilian life after six and a half years in the military. "Bob," my N.A. sponsor, was not happy because I had relapsed and it had cost me my military career. Bob, however, did state that perhaps civilian life would be better for me and that I could use my talents as a chef. He said, "In *ten years*, you'll own your own restaurant."

In 1995, I became a general manager for a chain of restaurants almost ten years to the day when "Bob" made that prediction. Although not technically the owner, I still had all the power of one. —*Anonymous*

"Bob's" spoken time line became an accurate prophecy—words which had been spoken and received when this man desperately needed hope.

Boss

Many people still harbor the image of a boss being a bad or mean person, cracking the whip and keeping well deserving people from a raise. Yet Nehemiah had a boss who loved him so much he gave him an unlimited leave of absence, and a draw upon the royal treasury, so that Nehemiah could follow his dream. It is not surprising that bosses can be a source of positive prophecy. In fact, in my first book, *Jesus, CEO,* I outline more than seventy-six ways good bosses can become more "prophet" oriented.

In the stories that follow, a casual remark or a sincere sentence of encouragement often becomes a form of prophecy, keeping an uncertain worker on her job, or shoring up the confidence of another.

I have been with Hewlitt Packard for fifteen years. I have a lot of passion for the company and believe in its roots. I was not aware that other people noted this.

One day I was attending a presentation on the "HP Way," i.e., the company culture, and I raised my hand to make a comment on how the founders of the company applied the HP Way. Just before I started, the general manager said, "Listen to him. If you want to see someone living the HP Way, here it is."

Since that comment, everything changed. I have become a

big speaker on the HP Way. I get a lot of requests to talk about it from other groups. —*R.R.*

The words spoken by this man's boss not only changed the way others viewed him, but also gave him a new perspective on himself.

I was working in South Carolina. I had graduated from the year before and it had taken me nine months to find a job. Finally, I landed one as a receptionist at a brokerage firm. After six months I had worked my way up to assistant branch manager. Soon after that I got a great job opportunity to go abroad and work in a branch office in Monte Carlo. At a little goodbye party right before I left, the branch manager raised his champagne glass and said, "Good luck, Kassie, I know I'm going to read about you someday!"

Ten years later, I was the feature of an article titled "Woman's Odyssey takes her from Kansas to Monte Carlo." I have since been named a "Woman to Watch" by the *Kansas City Star.* —*K.K.*

In this case, Kassie's prophet spoke with a glass raised in celebration. The spark of greatness he saw in her, he *spoke* to her, and she *heard* it.

While Working with Habitat for Humanity, a superior took me aside and said I could be a great wood trimmer for the house. He gave me two partners who also knew nothing about the job. Together we three women trimmed a whole house and did it well. We had a ball and learned a new skill and went on to learn many more building skills. Today I often am a crew chief on Habitat building sites.

Bosses and co-workers can often see God's spark of greatness in us. How blessed we are, and can be, when they declare the good that they see in us—to us.

Questions:

1. Which teacher has been a positive prophet in your life?

_____

_____

2. Why might God use a boss or a coworker to deliver a message to you about your future?

_____

_____

3. How can the words of professionals be used as sign posts for people?

_____

_____

4. Why do many people miss prophecies given to them by people in their everyday environment?

_____

_____

Meditation

Dear Lord,

You used Nehemiah's boss to help pave the way for his destiny.
You yourself were taught to read by teachers in the ancient Jewish
traditions. Help me be aware and alert to the professionals you
have placed in my world—to nurture me and strengthen me and
teach me in the way I should go. Likewise, let me be a guiding
light to everyone I know—at school, at work, at play, in my work
environment, and especially when I am counseling others one to
one.

   Amen

The Prophecy of Angels

*A*ngels have long been the appointed messengers of God—appearing first in the book of Genesis and last in the book of Revelations. One of my favorite stories about angels occurs in the book of Tobit, which is found in the New Jerusalem Bible.

The angel came into the house; Tobit greeted him, and the other answered, wishing him happiness in plenty. Tobit replied, "Shall I ever be happy again? I am a blind man; I no longer see the light of heaven; I am sunk in darkness like the dead who see the light no more." The angel said, "Take comfort; before long God will heal you. Take comfort." Tobit said, "My son Tobias wishes to go to Media. Will you join him as his guide? Brother, I will pay you." He replied, "I am willing to go with him; I know all the ways; I have often been to Media, I have crossed all its plains and moutains, and I know all its roads." Tobit said, "Brother, what family and what tribe do you belong to? Will you tell me, brother?" "What does my tribe matter to you?" the angel said. Tobit said, "I want to be quite sure whose son you are and what your name is." The angel said, "I am Azarias, son of the great Ananias, one of your kinsmen." "Welcome and greetings, brother! Do not be offended at my wanting to know the name of your family. I find you are my kinsman of a good and honourable line. I know Ananias and Nathan, the two sons of the great Shemaiiah. They used to go to Jerusalem with me; we have worshipped together there and they have never strayed from the right path. Your brothers are worthy men; you come of good stock, welcome." He went on. "I engage you at a drachma a day, with the same expenses as my own son's. Complete the journey with my son and I shall go beyond the agreed wage." The angel replied, "I shall complete the journey with him. Do not be afraid. On the journey outward all will be well; on the journey back all will be well; the road is safe." Tobit said, "Blessings on you, brother!" Then he turned to his son. "My child," he said, "prepare what you need for the journey, and set off with your brother. May God in heaven protect you abroad and bring you both back to me safe and sound! May his angel go with you and protect you, my child." The boy left with the angel, and the dog followed behind. *(Tobit 5; New Jerusalem Bible)*

Tobias proceeds safely to Media, and there he meets Sarah. Sarah, through the counsel of Raphael (Azarias), is freed from the grip of a terrible husband-murdering demon and falls in love with Tobias. So, Tobias returns home safely, not only with the silver, but also with the bride, which was his inheritance all along.

Tobias, Sarah, Tobit, and Anna, Tobit's wife, are preparing a huge wedding feast for the newcomers. Tobit plans to make good on his promise to his son's traveling companion, and calls him over to pay him. It is at this point that Raphael (Ananias) says, "I am going to tell you the whole truth, hiding nothing from you. You must know that when you and Sarah were at prayer, it was I who offered your supplications before the glory of the Lord and who read them; so too when you were burying the dead. God sent me to heal you and your daughter-in-law Sarah. I am Raphael, one of the seven angels who stand ever ready to enter the presence of the glory of the Lord." They were both overwhelmed with awe, they fell on their faces in terror. But the Angel said, "Do not be afraid; peace be with you. God bless you for ever. As far as I was concerned, when l was with you, my presence was not by any decision of mine, but by the will of God; he is the one whom you must bless as long as you live, he the one that you must praise. You thought you saw me eating, but that was appearance and no more. Now bless the Lord on earth and give thanks to God. I am about to return to him who sent me from above. Write down all that has happened." And he rose in the air. When they stood up again, he was no longer visible. They praised God with hymns; they thanked him for having performed such wonders; had not an angel of God appeared to them? *(Tobit 12 New Jerusalem Bible)*

I love this story for many reasons, not the least of which is the image of an angel, a young boy, and a dog setting off on a journey together. Tobit gives us a written example of how an angel became a prophet for God—appearing in answer to their prayers, and helping them overcome their largest problems. It is also interesting to note that the angel did not reveal himself as an angel until the very end. In fact, for most of the journey, he had an assumed name, and presented himself as a member of Tobit's own family. He seemed to eat and drink like a normal person, and even agreed to a salary for his wages. The message here is that not only can family members be angels in disguise, but so can coworkers. Do we heed, or ignore, their words?

Each person in the story had the advice of Raphael at different parts of their journey. By following the angel's instructions, they received their freedom—Tobit from his blindness and Sarah from her jealous demon. Raphael also presents a dramatic picture of angels appearing before God to plead the cases of humans. Jesus also mentioned this in Matthew 18:10, when he said, "See that you never despise any of these little ones, for I tell you that their angels in heaven are continually in the presence of my Father in heaven."

The angel's message to Tobit was that he knew the roads very well on the journey, both there and back, and that he would return his son safely to him. He also told him that God had heard his prayers, and seen his good works, and sent Raphael to help him.

Sometimes angels appear with halos, nine-feet wingspans and eyes of fire. And sometimes they might be a man with a knapsack on his back, traveling with a little dog.

One of God's favorite games is disguise. Treat everyone you meet with respect, for "many have entertained angels unawares."

Questions:

1. Has an angel ever spoken to you?

_____

_____

2. Do you know any people you suspect might really be angels of God in your life?

_____

_____

3. What do angels look like?

_____

_____

4. How do they act?

_____

_____

5. Why would God disguise angels as messengers among us?

_____

_____

Meditation

Dear Lord,
You sent Raphael to Tobit and his family disguised as a mere
mortal. Yet the words of Raphael proved to be pure wisdom to
those who listened. Please help me have an open and discerning
heart, quick to respond to the wisdom spoken to me through others
on your behalf.
  Amen

The Prophecy of Animals

$\mathcal{N}$o book on prophecy could be complete without examining all the ways God speaks to us, and scripture cites various references to animals being used to convey messages.

Here's a quick quiz. Who was the first false prophet in the Bible? The serpent. Adam just got through naming the animals when one of them showed up with a "false prophecy." And the serpent said to the woman, "Has God indeed said, You shall not eat of every tree of the garden?" And the woman said to the serpent, "We may eat of the fruit of the trees of the garden; but of the fruit of the tree which is in the midst of the garden, God has said, 'You shall not eat it, nor shall you touch it, lest you die.' " Then the serpent said to the woman, "You will not surely die. For God knows that in the day you eat of it your eyes will be opened, and you will be like God, knowing good and evil." *(Genesis 3:1–5)*

It is interesting to note that Jesus called the Scribes and Pharisees "broods of vipers." *(Matthew 12:34)* He considered them false prophets of the lowest order, because while they claimed their messages were from God, they were only enslaving people with laws they didn't keep themselves.

In fact, animals are used throughout scripture as symbols of good and evil, and are sometimes represented as active participants in the earthly drama. God commanded ravens to feed the prophet Elijah, and had hordes of quail dive bomb the complaining Israelites. *(I Kings 17:6, Numbers 11:31)*

God sent a dove to the Ark as a sign of his blessing. Balaam's donkey was allowed to speak and warn the misguided prophet that he was on the wrong road. One can assume that Jonah was not out surfing, but had to be at least semi-actively pursued by the great fish that swallowed him and became his retreat center when he was denying the call of God. A donkey willingly and loving carried a pregnant Mary to Jerusalem, and a donkey also waited patiently to give Jesus his last ride into the same city. The book of Revelations has so many animals in it it would make a zookeeper's head swim—each of them symbolizing some aspect of God or Satan.

This chapter is just a reminder that God can speak to us through animals—through the puppy that reminds us to laugh and engages us in a tug of war with a sock; through a kitten who sleeps contentedly curled up by the fire even though a storm is raging outside; through the birds that never seem to run out of songs, even though the newspapers might be reporting that the stock market is down.

Canaries used to be carried into mines to prophesy whether the air was safe. Groundhogs that see their shadows foretell an early spring. Trained dogs can determine when an epileptic is about to have a seizure, and the sudden flight of animals can often predict an earthquake.

Statistics show that people who have pets live longer, healthier, happier lives than those who do not. God has often used dolphins to rescue stranded swimmers, and golden retreivers are notorious for saving drowning children. I read last week about a cat who meowed and meowed to alert a groggy elderly couple that carbon monoxide was seeping into their home. It happens every day. Animals acting as messengers. Do we see it? Do we listen?

One day I let Miss Velvet, my quarterhorse mare, loose in a huge pasture. When I returned to bring her back into her stall I found her standing in a dry corner, her head leaning close to the radio a worker had left on in the field. Here she had so much space to roam, eat, and run, and her ears were tuned to the songs coming over the airwaves. Animals need and love to listen far more than we know.

In the book of Job, there is a beautiful rendition of a mighty creature, Leviathan, that practically shouts the name of God, just by "being."

I saw a picture of God on a postcard not too long ago. A huge polar bear was just awakening to the sunlight in a field of wildflowers. He held his massive paw up to shield the light from his eyes. I said to my friend, "That bear reflects God to me." When she asked me why, I replied, "Because of its unselfconscious magnificence." Sometimes animals prophesy just by "being."

Who would think God could use even a potbellied pig as a life-saving messenger?

Well, Edith does. Recently an article ran in several major newspapers about a potbellied pig who saved her owner's life. Edith had raised this pig as a house pet. It even had its own pet door to allow it easy access to the yard. One day Edith collapsed suddenly with a heart attack. She was too weak even to crawl to the next room to get the phone and dial 911. Never fear. Her pet pig was near. The pig dashed out the pet door and ran out into the road, where it proceeded to lie down with its legs sticking straight up in the air. Several cars just drove around it, but one young man stopped to see if he could render aid. As soon as he approached the pig, she leaped to her feet and ran towards the house where Edith lived. The young man followed, and as he neared the door he could hear Edith faintly calling for help. He was able to make the call, and Edith was saved.

Was this pig a messenger? Indeed, her actions became a form of prophecy for Edith.

God has messengers everywhere. May we learn to see them, and listen well to what they have to say.

Questions:

1. Has God ever spoken to you through an animal?

_____

_____

2. What was the message?

_____

_____

3. Did that message make a difference in your behavior?

_____

_____

4. Do a study of the symbolism of animals. Consider when you look at these creations what aspect of God may be being revealed.

_____

_____

Meditation

Dear Lord,

*Prophets are those who speak to us with words of encouragement,
and who are willing to tell the truth. Help me become more aware
of the honesty that is in animals—how they live without pretense
or shame. Help me recognize their divine connections to you, and
recognize them as the gifts they are to us—for companionship,
enjoyment, and assistance with our journey. You say that in
heaven the lion shall lie down with the lamb, and surely you enjoy
their comfort and personalities, too, or you would not have made
them. Let me treat all living things with respect, knowing I shall
meet them in heaven.*

Amen.

The Prophecy of Scripture

recent survey in *USA Today* revealed that 49 percent of Americans believe Biblical prophecies will come true, while a mere 16 percent put their trust in psychics. The challenge for those of us who love and read the Bible is understanding which prophecies to believe. Jesus spoke of signs and wonders to come, and also said that no one knew when The End would be. If you are reading this book after January 1, 2000, then obviously the millennium did not mark the end of the world. I am reminded of a sect leader from Japan who said that the world would end on a certain day in October of the year 1997, and claimed that this higher being would overtake the airwaves at exactly 12:00 noon to announce the next directions for the faithful. The media tuned in to this event with great anticipation, and I had to chuckle when at 12:00 noon the channel that the leader said would broadcast the message for the world showed Barney the dinosaur singing, "I love you, you love me, we are one big family." Perhaps that was God's idea of a joke—and not such bad advice, after all.

Prophets of gloom and doom abound, and partly that is true because if you want to gain a following there is no quicker way to do so than to announce a unifying cataclysmic event, or an enemy. I was on a radio show once with a preacher who truly wished he lived three thousand years ago. His favorite theme was death and destruction, and his words of condemnation were aimed particularly at people who disagreed with him.

I was trying to be as hospitable as I could, yet I had to take issue with him when he said that the King James Bible was the only true and accurate Word of God. I asked, "How could the King James Bible be the actual word of God when all historians and scholars agree that neither Moses nor Jesus spoke English?" He thought a moment, and then replied, "Jesus was bilingual!" I then reminded him that at one time the true and actual word of God was thought to be in Latin, and was to be kept only in the hands of a select few. "In fact, William Tyndale was put to death for having the audacity to tinker with the word of God by translating it from Latin into King James English," I said. This fact left the preacher momentarily speechless. Then his co-host piped up in his defense. "Well, I am teaching my children to speak Latin!" (This, no doubt, will bring all of us closer to the Lord.)

My point here is that words alone—no matter what language they are in—cannot convey the immensity of God. It took Jesus, and it takes us acting in his name, to do that. As Jesus says in Matthew 15:8, "These people worship me with their words, but their heart is far from me."

Many people have made a great deal of money writing and teaching about how to interpret biblical prophecies. I leave such elaborate interpretations of biblical signs and wonders to those inclined to study them, and who are more "bilingual."

Although 85 percent of Americans claim to have a Bible in their home, and 69 percent claim to read it weekly, 40 percent of those same people believed that Joan of Arc was Noah's wife. (She was not.) Perhaps we read the Bible "weakly," if at all.

When I spoke not too long ago at a seminar a woman raised her hand and asked how I had gained my knowledge of the Bible. I said simply, "I read it." That drew gales of laughter from the crowd, even though I hadn't intended it to be a facetious answer. Facilitators who come through our Path training seminars are often concerned at their lack of knowledge of some of the biblical stories. When one of them asked how to handle that concern, I gave him the same answer: "Read it."

Read it like a love story between God and us. Read it looking for the deeper messages hidden in the stories. Read it for therapy. Read it as a discipline. Memorize verses to sharpen your mind. Read it to try to understand God's heart. Yet above all, read it with wisdom and discernment.

I was surprised when on Bill Moyers's PBS special about "Genesis" one Jewish Rabbi said he will not let his daughter read the book of Genesis, because he does not want her to imprint that women were the ones who brought evil into the world.

In another theological discussion I overheard a preacher asking his instructor, "What is the message being conveyed when Sodom and Gomorrah is destroyed for being evil, yet Lot, the man who was saved, had just willingly offered up his two virgin daughters to be raped?" *(Genesis 19:6)*

Scriptures in the Old Testament are very clear that disobedient children are to be taken outside the city gates and stoned to death. Also "Everyone who curses his father or mother shall surely be put to death." *(Leviticus 20:9)*

Another scripture says that handicapped people are not to be allowed into the Temple to worship. "And the Lord spoke to Moses, saying, 'Speak to Aaron, saying "No man of your descendants in succeeding generations who has any defect may approach to offer the bread of his God. For any man who has a defect shall not approach; a man blind or lame, who has a marred face or any limb too long, a man who has a broken foot or broken hand, or is a hunchback or a dwarf, or a man who has a defect in his eye, or eczema or scabs or is a eunuch—he shall not go near the veil or approach the altar, because he has a defect, lest he profane My Sanctuaries." ' " *(Leviticus 21:16–23)*

Is this the word and will of God, or is it the reflection of certain cultural beliefs and prejudices at that time? (No wonder Jesus was so unpopular with the super-religious Scribes and Pharisees. Notice who most of his followers were—people who needed healing.)

Certainly, there are some passages in the Bible that contain mixed messages. At one point Jesus told a man to tell no one who he was. Yet at another point he tells his apostles to go and tell everyone what they have seen and heard. Which sentence was the truth?

Some people use the Bible like a Ouija board, flinging it open randomly, pointing to one scripture and then another to determine God's will. Heaven help them if they land on the scripture that says, "Judas went and hung himself," *(Matthew 27:5)* and then flip to another page that reads, "Go thou and do likewise." *(Luke 10:37)*

I submit these observations merely to caution against the use of written words to arbitrarily condemn and cauterize people.

I am constantly amazed at how people will pick and choose scriptures to make a point—particularly when it comes to gaining power or a sense of superiority over another person. Yet the one message that comes through clearly for me in both the Old and New Testaments is that humility is key to entering the gates of heaven, that judging others cuts us off from the very grace we need to breathe . . . that you will always find what you are looking for—either for good or for evil.

I am not blind to the evil all around us. I am aware that we wrestle with principalities and powers in realms beyond our knowing. Yet I am also aware that God, for whatever reason, has chosen to make us principal players on this stage—able to help direct and shape the future through our will, our ways, and our words. And that God's great desire is to bless us through the love of Christ.

"For I know the plans I have for you," declares the Lord, "plans to prosper you and not to harm you, plans to give you hope and a future." *(Jeremiah 29:11)*

"For I am convinced that neither death nor life, neither angels nor demons, neither the present nor the future, nor any powers, neither height nor depth, nor anything else in all creation, will be able to separate us from the love of God that is in Christ Jesus our Lord." *(Romans 8:38)*

These are the scriptures I believe.

There is a scripture that reads, "The testimony of Jesus is the spirit of prophecy." *(Revelations 19:10)*

As I have pondered what that verse means, I believe the woman's story that follows is its example. Regardless of all the nasty, negative predictions we have received, there is one true prophet to whom we all can turn.

My family and friends always told me how fat I was and that because I was so heavy I was a "waste of a beautiful woman." They said that I would go nowhere as far as a job was concerned, and as a woman that I could not find a man interested in me. One day Jesus spoke to me clearly. He said, "Come to me and I will give you all that you desire." Today, Jesus shows me through his words that I am beautiful in His sight, holy and pure, and that my future husband will love me as He loves the church. I know now that I am accepted into eternal life in Heaven just like I am. *Jesus was a true prophet to me.* —D.P.

In my mind, all scriptures point ultimately to one prophecy. If we believe the testimony of Jesus, our entire lives, and our destiny, will be changed.

Questions:

1. Which scriptures have become prophecies for you?

_____

_____

2. What is your feeling about the Bible? How often do you read it? What do you read?

_____

_____

3. How could the study of the Bible help lead someone to a deeper understanding of God's will?

_____

_____

4. What are the dangers of using scriptures to condemn others?

_____

_____

5. Why do you think so many people like to do it anyway?

_____

_____

Meditation

Dear Lord,
I thank you for your words in my life, and for the scriptures which
detail the love story you have for us. Help me read your words
with love and wisdom and discernment. Set your words upon my
mouth and heart and tongue, so that I may reflect your wisdom in
all I say and do.
    Amen

The Prophecy of Dreams and Visions

$\mathcal{D}$reams are an important way of hearing the voice of God. In scripture we learn that dreams and visions were sometimes viewed as being one and the same. The entire fate of Christianity was shaped through visions, prophecy, and dreams.

Mary was told by an angel in a vision that she was going to have a child. "Rejoice, the Lord is with you," said Gabriel. "You have won God's favor, and you are to conceive and have a child, and you must name him Jesus." *(Luke 1:28)*

In fact, the fate of the little baby depended entirely on Mary and Joseph listening to angels and believing the dreams they were being given.

"Behold, an angel of the Lord appeared to Joseph in a dream, saying, 'Arise, take the young child and his mother, flee to Egypt, and stay there until I bring you word; for Herod will seek the young child to destroy him.' When he awoke, he took the young child and his mother by night and departed for Egypt, and was there until the death of Herod, that it might be fulfilled which was spoken by the Lord through the prophet, saying, 'Out of Egypt I called My Son.' " *(Matthew 2: 13–14)*

Joseph's response was so immediate to this dream that he arose and took them that night to Egypt. His obedience also helped fulfill a larger prophecy—one that had predicted the temporary geographical location of Jesus.

What if Joseph had not listened when warned in a dream to take sudden flight to Egypt, sparing the life of his infant son from the desperate sword of Herod's executioners? The father of Judaism itself, Abraham, heard God speak to him through dreams and visions. Dreams were one of the main ways God communicated to a nomadic tribe, many of whom could not read. Fortunately for all of us, they could believe, and acted on their dreams.

Pilate's wife also had a dream, which her husband chose to ignore. In this scene, Jesus is facing Pilate, having been brought before him by the chief priests and the elders.

"Now at the feast the governor was accustomed to releasing to the multitude one prisoner who they wished. At that time they had a notorious prisoner called Barabbas. Therefore, when they had gathered together, Pilate said to them, 'Whom do you want me to release to you? Barabbas, or Jesus who is called Christ?' For he knew that they had handed Him over because of envy.

"While he was sitting on the judgment seat, his wife sent to him, saying, 'Have nothing to do with that just Man, for I have suffered many things today in a dream because of Him.' "

But the crowd continued to shout for Barabbas. Finally, "When Pilate saw that he could not prevail at all, but rather that a tumult was rising, he took water and washed his hands before the multitude, saying, 'I am innocent of the blood of this just Person. You see to it.' Then he released Barabbas to them, and when he had scourged Jesus, he delivered Him to be crucified." (Matthew 27:11–26)

All of Pilate's hand washing did not erase the blood from his hands. If he had only heeded his wife's dream, rather than "the tumult of the crowd," his place in history would have been a totally different one.

Sometimes dreams offer visions of the future.

For example, a young brother had a series of dreams, that charted his destiny. Now Joseph had a dream and he told it to his brothers; and they hated him even more. So he said to them, "Please hear this dream which I have dreamed: There we were, binding sheaves in the field. Then behold, my sheaf arose and also stood upright, and indeed your sheaves stood all around and bowed down to my sheaf." And his brothers said to him, "Shall you indeed reign over us? Or shall you indeed have dominion over us?" So they hated him even more for his dreams and for his words.

Then he dreamed still another dream and told it to his brothers, and said, "Look, I have dreamed another dream. And this time the sun, the moon, and the eleven stars bowed down to me." So he told it to his father and his brothers; and his father rebuked him and said to him, "What is this dream that you have dreamed? Shall your mother and I and your brothers indeed come to bow down to the earth before you?" And his brothers envied him, but his father kept the matter in mind. *(Genesis 37: 5–10)*

What follows is a soap opera of sibling rivalry. The brothers conspire to kill Joseph. "They said to one another, 'Look, this dreamer is coming! Let us kill him and cast him into some pit; and we shall say, "Some wild beast has devoured him." We shall see what will become of his dreams!' But Reuben heard it, and he delivered him out of their hands, and said, 'Let us not kill him. Shed no blood, but cast him into this pit which is in the wilderness and do not lay a hand on him,' that he might deliver him out of their hands, and bring him back to his father." *(Genesis 37:19–21)*

One of the brothers gets an even better idea. (These guys were kind of like the Hardy Boys of Jerusalem.) He decides that they should sell Joseph to some passing traders, which is indeed what they do. Thus, Joseph does *not* have his brothers bowing down to him—but instead is being led off by foreigners into slavery.

Joseph not only had dreams, but he also was given the power to interpret them. This gift helped Joseph rise from slavery and move into the position of head administrator for Pharaoh. He interprets one of Pharaoh's dreams as a warning from God that seven years of plenty will be followed by seven years of famine. Pharaoh was wise enough to heed this dream, and gave Joseph the authority to begin saving wheat.

Ultimately, the famine affects everyone. Near starvation, Jacob sends his sons to go to Egypt to try to find food. It must have been quite a scene when the brothers who had sold him into slavery were now bowing before him, asking him for the grain which only he had the power to give.

Joseph's dream proved to be prophetic.

My editor urged me to share a few of the personal dreams and visions that have helped guide me on my spiritual journey, and in recollecting what these were, I realized anew how important these dreams have been as a means of expressing God's voice and will for me.

When I first began to feel uncomfortable in the realm of advertising (due to my yearning to write about more spiritual matters), I had a dream which revealed a passage away from the demands of worldly success which my father so desperately craved for me, and towards the mystical, intangible work I really wanted to do.

In this particular dream I saw myself dressed in a genie's outfit, lying on a pitcher's mound. Through the chain link fence an old man with a few scraggly hairs on his head was poking his skeletal fingers at me, and screaming at the top of his lungs, "PLAY BALL! I SAID PLAY BALL!" In the dream I slowly stood up, faced the old man, and said, "I don't want to play ball anymore. I am a genie," and then turned and walked off the field.

This dream gave me permission to leave what I had been doing, "playing ball" to please my father, and walk toward a new field of action. The genie's outfit was important because it signified that God had clothed me for a different kind of work. Had I not had that outfit, I might not have felt ready to walk off the field. Somehow the costume gave me courage (even though I didn't much care for the shoes).

Another dream which has been so significant to me came right before I wrote *The Path: Creating Your Mission for Work and for Life*. In this dream I saw a poised and quiet woman standing by a turquoise pool. She was wearing a long white flowing robe and was barefoot. The setting was full of pink sunset clouds and white pillars, much like a Maxfield Parrish painting. As I watched her I noticed that she was looking down at a number of fish which were flopping around at her feet.

She reached down, and began picking them up one at a time and putting them back in the water. She was very gentle as she did this, being careful not to damage their scales. The fish made a happy swishing noise and then swam away.

I said, "Lord, I want to be that woman!" I heard a voice say, "You will be," just as I awoke.

The fish out of water symbolized people who are literally gasping for breath, like so many people who are out of their element. If they only knew what God created them to do, they could get back to being productive and happy. I desperately wanted the satisfaction of being able to help return the fish to water. I noticed that the woman in the dream had no shoes, meaning she was vulnerable, and that she was not kicking the fish back into the water, although that might have seemed like the fastest and easiest thing to do.

As I work with people now, and see the joy on their faces as suddenly the meaning and context of their mission in life becomes clear, I am reminded of that dream, and I know I am doing the right thing.

Dreams sometimes offer visions of the future.

One of my readers sent in a story in which as a child he would often draw up charts of Bible stories, and he would "see" these people sitting in front of him, taking notes and writing down what he had to say. He grew up to be a pastor, and he says that one day as he was giving a sermon, he suddenly recognized the people in front of him as being the exact people he had seen in his mind as a child twenty years before. "You are not new to me," he told the congregation. "I saw you in my dreams many years ago."

Steve couldn't sleep at night. He kept hearing the sounds of babies crying. He would get up and go check on his three children, and come back to bed and tell his wife, Kathy, "I keep hearing children crying but they are not ours." Finally in desperation he asked God to help him—he was losing sleep every night. Then he heard a voice say, "The crying that you hear is from the sounds of my children in Mexico. Get up and go help them. They have no father or mother." So Steve and Kathy left their church in Michigan and moved to Juarez, Mexico, and began working with orphaned children. They are now building a home called Casa de las Jemas (House of Jewels), which will house, clothe, train, and feed 250 orphans. Steve said, "As soon as I took action, the sounds of the crying stopped."

Sometimes people are given almost simultaneous dreams and visions as in the case of Cornelius and Paul recounted in Acts Chapter 10. Both men, very different, had related dreams within a 24-hour period. Cornelius, a Roman centurion, had a vision of an angel "about the ninth hour of the day" telling him to "send men to Joppa, and send for Simon whose surname is Peter. He is lodging with Simon, a tanner, whose house is by the sea. He will tell you what you must do." And when the angel who had spoken to him had departed, Cornelius called two of his household servants and a devout soldier from among those who had waited on him continually. So when he had explained all these things to them, he sent them to Joppa.

"The next day, as they went on their journey and drew near the city, Peter went up on the housetop to pray, about the sixth hour. Paul fell into a trance and saw heaven opened and an object like a great sheet bound at the four corners, descending to him . . ." The sheet contains all kinds of unclean animals. A voice commands Peter to eat the food. Peter, in horror, declines, saying, "Lord, I have never eaten anything common or unclean." And a voice spoke to him again the second time, saying, "What

God has cleansed you must not call unclean." This was done three times, and then the sheet was taken up into heaven again.

The dreams of these two men ultimately change religious history, for when Cornelius's men approach Peter and beckon him to return with them to the home of an unclean "centurion," Peter agrees to go with them. It is there, in Caesarea, that he realizes for the first time that God is sending him to preach grace and acceptance to the formerly unclean Romans, and others who were not born of Jewish blood. (*Acts Chapter 10*)

I think we underestimate the courage of Peter in choosing to believe a dream over all scriptural and historical precedent at that time. There were no scriptures telling him, or anyone, that it was okay to mingle or mix with the Gentiles. In fact, all the known scriptures pointed otherwise. Yet I believe that Peter was able to have faith in this dream because he had spent time with Jesus, and knew his heart. It was the strength of his personal relationship with Christ that opened the door to the gospel to those of us who were not born Jews. We should all be grateful that Peter believed a dream.

Dee Jones, my administrator, shares a story about a powerful simultaneous dream she had with her four-year-old son.

I struggled to consciousness from a deep sleep. As my sleepy fog cleared, a horrible realization dawned. In my dead-tired state, I must have dozed off, leaving my four-year-old son in the bathtub. Panic rising in my body, I jumped out of bed and tore down the hall toward the bathroom. The hall seemed very long. I couldn't run, as if some invisible force was holding me back. My feet seemed mired in the hall carpet which was turning into soft brown earth beneath me. Suddenly, the walls of the hall fell away and a row of ancient-looking trees took their place, waving ominously in the breeze as I passed. As I labored toward the bathroom door, it too disappeared, and in its place, a huge meadow filled with tall grass appeared. As I ran to the edge of the clearing, where the bathtub should have been, I found a deep, dark pit, filled with water. At the bottom of the pit, lay my lifeless four-year-old son, Brett. I dove in, wrapped my arms around him, heart beating wildly, and swam for the surface.

I bolted upright in my bed, gasping for breath. It was three in the morning. The house was quiet. The only sound I could hear was my heart pounding in my chest. I was disoriented. I had been dreaming, yet it was such a vivid dream. So real, in fact, that I arose and walked quickly down the hall, first, to check the bathtub. It was empty. Next, I went into my son's room where I found him sleeping peacefully in his bed. Satisfied that it had really been a dream, I returned to bed and fell into a deep slumber.

The morning dawned much like any other. I arose, made coffee, dressed for work, prepared breakfast, packed Brett's lunch for his preschool—the normal routine. Brett met me with a smile as I woke him. His first words were, "Mommy, I had a dream." I found this statement rather remarkable, since I didn't think we'd ever discussed dreams, but we were running late and I didn't really pay much attention to him. "Oh, that's nice," I said. "You can tell me about it tonight, okay?" "Okay, Mom," he chirped happily. And with that we went on with our day.

That evening, when I picked him up from preschool, the first thing out of his mouth was, "Mom, I've got to tell you about my dream." This must have been some dream, I thought, for him to keep it in focus since the morning. He began, "I was at the bottom of this deep, dark pit, filled with water." His statement took my breath away. "You were?" I managed to answer. "What happened next?" "A mermaid saved me, she swimmed down and wrapped me in her arms and taked me up," he replied. "What happened next?" I asked. "I don't know, I waked up," he said, "but Mom, I really love the mermaid."

This dream demonstrates the inexplicable bond parents have with their children—a bond which transcends space and time.

My mother demonstrated her ability to see over the miles when I was seventeen. I had just graduated from high school and moved to Washington, D.C., for the summer, where I was privileged to work in a congressional office. Mom and Dad agreed that we would talk every Friday night at 7:00 P.M. to catch up on my activities. One hot sultry night I was sitting on the stoop of my boarding house, watching people walk by, when a very handsome man with a French accent came up and started talking to me. One doesn't hear too many French accents where I grew up, so I was instantly enchanted by this man who had curly black hair, piercing blue eyes, and a debonair manner.

When he offered to show me the monuments, I unhesitatingly went with him. Unfortunately, we drove not to the monuments but to his house. At this point I began to get suspicious, and when he led me into a living room that was full of life-size photographs of nude women, I knew I was in trouble. He locked the door behind us, and went outside to the backyard, where he pulled some clean white sheets off of the line. He then pulled me close to him and asked, "How do you like my pictures?" As I whispered, "I don't," I began furiously looking for routes of escape. Just then the phone rang. He went into the kitchen to answer it, and I shot out the still opened back door like a rocket. I scrambled over the fence and began running down the alley as fast as my legs would carry me. I happened to glance at my watch as I was running. It was 7:19 P.M. I ran down several blocks and then hopped on a bus and made my way back to the boarding house.

There, on my door, was a message from the front desk. "Laurie, your mother called. Wednesday, 7:19 P.M." After I had calmed down I called.

"Honey, are you all right?" Mom cried. "Of course I am, Mom. Why do you ask?" "Well, I was standing here doing the dishes when suddenly I got an image of you running down an alley like you were in danger." "Oh, Mom, I'm fine. I was just out seeing the town, that's all." Only years later did I share with her the accuracy of her vision.

Vision is the ability to transcend time as we know it. Sometimes we can do this through prayer and meditation.

A young woman told me at the beginning of my seminar that she was trying to decide whether to stay in San Diego and marry her boyfriend, or go back to Washington, D.C., to practice law. Of course, I had no immediate information or answers for her. When we did the vision exercise, however, I asked everyone to simply close their eyes and imagine that it is now Monday morning, 9:00 A.M., three years from today. "What are you wearing?" I asked. "What do you see in front of you? Who are you meeting for lunch?" The young woman gasped audibly.

When the exercise was complete I asked her what had happened. She said, "I saw myself so clearly. I was wearing a business suit, carrying a briefcase, and walking up the steps to the Capitol building. It was as if I had already done it!" Her vision gave her the answer.

Another woman in one of our Path seminars declared in her vision of what she would be doing three years from now that she would be spending more time with her husband and children in a resort location, eating lunch with him at a leisurely pace. She saw herself working in leisure clothes, as opposed to the power dressing she currently did; being home when the girls arrived from school, having weeknight dinners with her husband, as opposed to having him coming home late after work. To her amazement, her vision came true within ninety days of writing it down. Her husband was transferred in a surprising way to a resort location, and with the reduced workload, the whole family began to frolic on the beach, as written in her vision. Her three-year-forward self became real in ninety days.

Sometimes a vision can be one that is brought into reality only by strength and determination.

Not so long ago New York City seemed to have lost its vision. With one of the nation's highest crime rates, slum rates, city debts, and business taxes New York was on the verge of bankruptcy. In a somewhat apt metaphor there was a barge floating through the harbor filled with garbage that was not allowed to land. Nobody wanted New York's garbage—not even New York. But then, something happened. The City got a new vision under the leadership of Rudolph Giuliani. Citizens banded together. Congress passed a bill allowing all cities to put more cops on the street. Policemen got smarter, and tougher, taking a preventative approach to crime through neighborhood patrols and inner city relationships.

In perhaps one of the most telling stories of the determination of a mayor to change the future of a city drowning in blood, Mayor Rudolph Giuliani declared a zero tolerance for crime. He asked to be notified every time a murder took place in the city, no matter what time of night or day. He kept a clipboard with him at all times and when the different boroughs reported in, he would ask the police chief in charge, "How could this murder have been prevented?" Within a short period of time the murder rate was cut in half. Economics improved, as well, and New York City went from being an example of one of the most debt-ridden, least desirable cities in the world to the number one desired vacation spot in the world, with a $1.2 billion dollar surplus. This was not an accident or a fluke of nature. It took leaders of vision, willing to write the vision down.

In the book *Higher Creativity* by Willis Harman and Howard Rheingold, the story is told of Ramanujan, a child who became one of the leading mathematicians of the twentieth century and the first Indian to be elected to the Royal Society of London. When his genius came to the attention of Cambridge scholars, the boy's mother refused to allow her son to leave India. However, one morning the mother announced that she had had a dream on the previous night, in which she saw her son seated in a big hall amidst a group of Europeans, and that she had been told by a voice in the night not to stand in the way of fulfilling her son's purpose. He was allowed to go to England, and indeed her dream came true.

There have been an amazing "coincidence" of movies and books preceding events which actually took place. While producers were filming the sci-fi adventure about an asteroid hitting earth, NASA announced that it had suddenly discovered a mile-wide asteroid bound for earth. The next day it recalculated the figures to show that it would not actually come within striking distance, yet I can't help but wonder if the power of a written script caused the event to become a current news headline.

In the book *Brave New World* by Aldous Huxley, he foresaw a state which had video cameras everywhere watching the citizens, and laboratories where babies were created in test tubes. This book was written in 1932, long before such events were realities.

Gene Roddenberry in his prescient *Star Trek* novels foresaw many of the technologies we have today, including holographic images which had not yet been created. Now you can find them in any postcard shop.

Perhaps we need to reassess the powers of our fiction.

Perhaps writers, setting sails in the seas of creative drift, are stumbling onto shores of future realities. Perhaps our poets are our prophets.

We need to pay attention to our dreams, and listen to the messages contained within our visions.

When I was living in Dallas in the early 1970s, I and a small band of my friends were working on creating what I called The Rainbow Dream. This was going to be a noble undertaking of spreading God's love through books and songs and movies. One of my friends decided that we would need a place for our head-quarters. She came back after a morning drive one day and said, "I've found it. Come and see." We drove out together, with her little dog Skipper between us, and twenty minutes out into the country she pulled up off the road near some rural street signs marked Love Drive and Royal Lane. Gentle green rolling hills stretched out as far as we could see. Only a rabbit hopping by and an occasional bird joined us as I excitedly began to draw plans in the dirt. "Right here will be the Communications Center," I said, "and over there will be some hotels, because people will be flying in to visit us, of course. And there, over to the left, we'll have some stables so everyone can ride their horses on their lunch breaks and after work." We hurried back to town so I could draw out the plans on paper. My friend even went to the County Recorder's Office to see who owned it. "Some farmer," she said, "but it's not for sale."

I was working as a baby-sitter at the time. Linda was a waitress. Billy was a waiter. Larry Gene was working at a frame shop, and Edwin was working at Southwest Airlines. Between us we could barely afford the rent for our small apartments. But the plans went down on paper, and I have the copies still.

Well, the Rainbow began to fade after a couple of years, and we all went our separate ways. Billy stayed in Dallas, and we kept in touch. One day he called me, about ten years after we had said our Rainbow goodbyes. "You have to come and see this," he said. I flew out to visit and he took me for a ride in his car. We drove out along Love Drive, which by now had become more developed. As we pulled up near the corner of Love Drive and Royal Lane, I gasped. There stood The Dallas Communications Center, a huge multi-acre complex for writers and animators and recording artists and screenwriters. Across the way, on the left, was a beautiful Equestrian Center, complete with air-conditioned stalls. And over behind the Center, just as I had drawn, were numerous hotels. I felt a mixture of sadness, anger, relief, and joy.

"Someone stole our dream!" I said. "No, Laurie," Billy said. "God just took it to someone who could afford it."

"I walk out, I see something, some event that would otherwise have been utterly missed and lost; or something sees me, some enormous power brushes me with its clean wing, and I resound like a beaten bell," writes Annie Dillard in *Pilgrim at Tinker Creek*.

Some enormous power had brushed me with its clean wing that day, when I was standing with my friends in an open field in Dallas. I had been given a vision of what was to come.

I have also received another vision, which I believe is coming true even as I write this.

The year was 1972. I was working as a substitute teacher in a one-room school house in a place called Weed, New Mexico. As I was driving my little Datsun pickup truck home, a song came on the radio about a drug dealer promising that "things will feel better" if you "just call." All my little fourth graders knew that song, and could recite it word for word. I was haunted by this fact, and when the song came on the radio in my car as I was driving home I put my right hand on the radio and prayed. "Lord, why should songs about drug dealers be number one on the radio? Shouldn't your words and songs be on the lips of our children? This isn't right. I promise I will do whatever I can to help change this dynamic. I believe that the airwaves should be a means of distributing your light and love, and not celebrating the powers of darkness." Suddenly a vision appeared in my mind. I saw the gates of Jerusalem surrounded by people clothed in rags. They were scrawling obscenities on the walls. Just then the gates began to open and a light more powerful than any I had ever

seen came bursting through. I shouted in glee at the vision, because to me it meant that the lower life forms would have their
day, but God would ultimately triumph.

I shared my vision with one of my friends at church, who
suggested that I meet with some people in El Paso who were
forming a new Christian television station. At the meeting I was
greeted warmly. Charlie, the main man, said, "Before our meeting I was praying and the Lord told me to have you read this
passage before we start." "What is it?" I asked. He pointed to
Psalm 24 verses 7–10, and I read in awe the following words—
words which I had not seen before.

> Lift up your heads, O you gates!
> And be lifted up, you ancient doors!
> And the King of glory shall come in.
> Who is this King of glory?
> The Lord, strong and mighty,
> the Lord, mighty in battle.
> Lift up your heads, O you gates!
> And be lifted up, O ancient doors
> And the King of glory shall come in.

When I asked him what these words meant to him, he said,
"We don't know, exactly. We were told you would explain."

That vision and confirmation meeting took place almost thirty
years ago. Has anything changed? People are still scrawling obscenities on the walls. Yet as I sit here the number one song on
the airwaves is about a father loving his little girl. One of the top
television series is *Touched by an Angel*. And more and more parents are sending their children to parochial schools, or home

schooling them, so they can monitor more closely the songs that are sung on the playground.

At a recent conference I attended scientific experts were predicting that soon all our technologies will be based on light. Fiber optics and satel-"lite" transmissions are fast becoming the main means of disseminating intelligence and information, as well as entertainment. My prayer is that soon all of our airwaves will be filled with light, and the King of Glory shall come in.

So, I have hope that this vision is coming true. And meanwhile I am doing my part to help influence what is being written and transmitted to the human eye and ear and heart.

How do we know things that cannot yet be known? The average soy plant has four billion root hairs per square inch, when viewed under the microscope. Perhaps our souls are like that, with billions of root hairs tuned into the mind of God, only most of us don't know that. Or more of us would be prophets.

When we are in the womb our vestibule nerves are centered in our ear drums. The entire nervous system develops out of that locale, and in those early stages the only information we receive as a fetus is movement. Perhaps the hunch, or the quickening of breath, or the peace we suddenly feel has to do with an early inner knowing. "You were there when I was being formed in utter seclusion! You saw me before I was born, and scheduled each day of my life before I began to breathe. Every day was recorded in your Book! *(Psalm 139:15–16)*

John C. Maxwell, author of *Developing the Power Within You,* writes, "Success is due in large part to your personal vision." Walt Disney had already died when Disney World first opened, so his widow was asked to speak. She was introduced by a man who said, "Mrs. Disney, I just wish Walt could have seen this."

She stood up, said with a smile, "He did," and sat down. Visions are powerful.

Surely, the mind of God sees all our possibilities. We need to learn to see them, too.

Questions:

1. Have you ever had a dream or a vision which later came true?

_____

_____

2. What was it?

_____

_____

3. Do you have recurring dreams?

_____

_____

4. How could God speak to you today?

_____

_____

5. Draw a picture of your concept of time. Is it a line? A box? A square? A circle? Waves?

_____

_____

6. Put yourself somewhere in that picture. Where are you "in time"?

_____

_____

7. Put God in it.

_____

_____

8. File a "Flight Plan" for your life. Pretend that you are a pilot. Write down where you are headed, the path you plan to take, and when you are scheduled to arrive.

_____

_____

Meditation

Dear Lord,
Speak your will into my life through a vision or dream. Keep me
open to see the symbolism in everything around me. Make me
keenly aware of your ability to speak to me through any means
necessary to guide me towards my destiny. Help me remember and
understand my dreams, and not dismiss them. Give me people
who are able to help me discern and interpret images and visions
which I receive. Help me keep your vision for me, as someone
destined to rule with you, always in my mind.
*   Amen.*

Section III

How to Prophesy

Tips on Cultivating and Sharing the Gift

How to Prophesy

"Above all else, seek the gift of prophecy."
I Corinthians 14:1

The role of the prophet is a sacred and hallowed one, revered in all major religions as a valid means of helping groups and individuals discern their destiny. The intention of this book is to help each of us accept the responsibility of speaking words which teach and encourage and challenge one another to a higher level of seeing and being. Prophecy is not only knowing the mind of God—it is also about knowing yours—how it works, what it believes, what it is consciously and subconsciously pulling you toward.

I feel compelled here to offer a brief background and overview of prophecy from the Judeo-Christian perspective, some of which has been gleaned from the *Illustrated Bible Dictionary* and *Jerome's Bible Commentary*.

The Jewish people were unique among other ancient peoples in that the Jews worshiped only one God, not many, and believed that prophetic events could indicate that God had a change of mind or heart. All other religions at that time saw their gods as implacable and immutable, unmoved by new information. Thus, prophecy for the Jews became a way of discerning the mind of an active and observant God who was personally concerned with their welfare.

Prophets spoke the words of God as revealed to them in a variety of ways. It could be through dreams and visions, a direct personal awareness or sense of illumination, and could involve being in a state of individual or group ecstasy. Some prophets had secretaries, like Jeremiah *(Jeremiah 36:4)*, and some had disciples, like Isaiah *(Isaiah 8:16)*. Some had a reputation of knowing what was said in secret from afar, like Elisha *(2 Kings 6:12)*. Every prophet had a distinct personality or temperament which shone through their prophecies. Jeremiah is sometimes referred to as the weeping prophet. Isaiah seemed to be able to find good in any disaster. Many of them were reluctant and considered themselves untalented, like Amos and Jeremiah *(Amos 3:7–8, Jeremiah 1:7–8)*.

Some prophets were not above giving false information if the price was right, like Balaam *(Numbers 22:5–35)* and the prophets of King Jehosophat *(1 Kings 22:5–12)*.

Samuel, Nathan, and Amos enjoyed the benefits of being paid for their professional duties as prophets, while others did not.

Jesus accepted the title of prophet, as well as teacher and healer, before he accepted any other.

Music and ritual dance were sometimes accompanied by prophecies, and at one time the temple singers were also considered prophets themselves.

False prophets also arose up and tried to direct people according to their own agendas.

The hallmarks of false prophets were that they called you after other gods rather than the one true God, and eventually bore evil fruit themselves.

Sometimes false prophets predicted things that came true, which was meant to serve as a test for God's people to see who they would follow and serve.

Sometimes God's prophets spoke the truth, and sometimes

they spoke out of their own agendas, as when Peter asked Jesus not to go to Jerusalem, and Moses brought water out of the rock without seeking God's permission.

Jesus saw himself as the ultimate prophet, and then predicted that the Holy Spirit would pour out a spirit of prophecy on a multitude of believers, from generation to generation.

With this as a backdrop, let us then with great respect examine how we might rise to the level of prophecy which is our inheritance, and claim it, even as we recognize the various levels of prophecy which occur in our society today.

Prophecy is a gift that can also be cultivated. If you desire to prophesy, pray earnestly that you may receive it. And while you pray, you might also want to do the following.

Twelve Steps to Becoming a Prophet

1. **Keep good company**. The only self-declared prophet I ever met was at a Spiritual CEO conference in the Bahamas. He told the sponsor that the Lord had told him to come to the conference, and when one of the invited keynote speakers failed to show due to travel problems, this man jumped on the podium and began to prophesy. First his prophecies were about the Bahamas, but it quickly turned to people in the audience. Based on the information that he called out about me, he was fairly good at it. Although he had never met me, he knew that I was a writer. His prophecy that I was about to be called in for consulting with governors and kings came true when two months later I was invited to speak and pray with

generals and other leading officers at the Pentagon. He also told me that a manuscript I had been working on for years needed to come to fruition. (It has.)

I later checked with other people in the crowd over whom he prophesied, and learned that he had been incredibly accurate with them. There was a young woman in his entourage who prophesied as well, not with the same confidence, but with startling accuracy. He informed me that he had been training her, and that he could train me, too. When I asked him how, he said, "Remember the story of Saul in the Bible who came upon a group of prophets and began prophesying himself? It's the same principle. If you get around people who are doing it, you too will suddenly find the ability within yourself." *(Samuel 10:5-8)*

King David and King Solomon wrote often about the importance of keeping the company of good counselors. In fact, in the very first Psalm David declares, "Blessed is the one who walketh not in the counsel of the ungodly, nor standeth in the way of sinners, nor sitteth in the seat of the scornful." *(Psalm 1:1)*

We can be blessed, or cursed, by the company we keep. More often than not you can predict what a person will become by looking at who he or she hangs around with.

2. *Seek wisdom.* "If any person lacks wisdom, let him or her ask for it," writes Paul in his letter to the young apostle James. *(James 1:5)*

Solomon describes Wisdom as a feminine force so lovely that "in her company all good things came to me. For when life is shared with her, there is no sorrow—only peace and joy." He continues:

Wisdom I loved and searched for from my youth: I
　resolved to have
her as my bride. I fell in love with her beauty.
She enhances her noble birth by sharing God's life,
for the Master of all has always loved her.
Indeed, she shares the secrets of God's knowledge,
and she chooses what he will do.
If in this life wealth is a desirable possession, who
is more wealthy than wisdom, whose work is everywhere?
Or if it be the intellect that is at work, who, more than
　she,
designs whatever exists?
Or if it be uprightness you love,
why, virtues are the fruit of her labours,
since it is she who teaches temperance and prudence,
justice and fortitude;
nothing in life is more useful for human beings.
Or if you are eager for wide experience,
she knows the past, she forecasts the future,
she knows to turn maxims, and solve riddles;
she has foreknowledge of signs and wonders,
and the unfolding of signs and wonders,
and the unfolding of the ages and the times.

　　　　　　　—Wisdom 8:2–8 The New Jerusalem Bible

　　When Solomon was asked what gift he would most like in
all the world, he asked for wisdom.

　　Psalm 1 says "His delight is in the law of the Lord, and in
his law he doth meditate day and night." The result of this is

"that he shall be like a tree planted by the rivers of water, that bringeth forth fruit in its season. His leaf shall not wither, and whatsoever he doeth shall prosper." *(Psalm 1:2–3)*

This advice comes with a powerful positive prophecy. The person that seeks to know the mind and heart of God, meditating on it both day and night, will thrive and prosper. How simple can it get?

Scholars of leadership skills now believe that those people who are able to predict and understand human behavior will always outpace those who merely follow the crowd. The study of wisdom is the study of the mind of God and the heart of humankind. What field of study could be more profitable—or interesting? I now understand the ancient Jews who longed more than anything to be able to study the Torah all day long. The word of God is such sweet food for the soul.

3. ***Anticipate outcomes.*** People who are able to prophesy or predict events are really just reporting anticipated outcomes. They are able to sense patterns of thought or behavior which, if unchanged, will lead to a probable event.

One of my favorite stories about anticipation consists of a group of animal rescue workers. Several people in the community have purchased low frequency receivers which can pick up the radio frequency of the "dog catcher." So, when a call goes out, "We have a report of a stray wandering around on Hamilton Avenue," one of the people will dash into their car and run down to that part of town, often getting the dog before the dog catcher does. These team members have a sophisticated network of information and anticipation. Explaining this covert operation to me, one of the women explained,

"We don't feel like we're doing anything wrong, because the dog is just a stray. Once the dog catcher has it, it becomes a prisoner—usually doomed to die."

Wouldn't it be nice if we had high frequency scanners which could predict a child about to get into trouble long before the police have to be called in? Anticipation and prevention are perhaps the most effective forms of prophecy. Alexander Weir III of the San Diego city schools has devoted more than twenty years to kids who have become parents too early, after having become one himself. He developed a program called MARCH—Males Acting Responsibly for Community Health, which takes in boys that are at risk for joining gangs or becoming early parents. It puts them to work in after school sessions, teaching them self-esteem, goal-setting, and how to avoid negative situations. He is a prophet working to prevent negative futures from happening.

El Paso has a prophetic program that runs every New Year's Eve. Volunteers come in and take calls from all over town, dispatching free cab rides to people who are too drunk to drive. One young man who has been volunteering at the program for the last four years was asked why he would give up his own New Year's Eve celebration to sit by a bank of phones for twelve hours. "Knowing that maybe one more person, or even a family, is alive because I took a call and got someone a cab is the best New Year's present I could ever give myself," he said. In the five years since the program has been initiated, El Paso has not experienced one traffic fatality on that holiday night. This is positive, anticipatory prophecy at work.

According to a report in the *Atlantic Monthly* entitled "The

Prison-Industrial Complex," Eric Schlosser reports that approximately *seventy percent of all prison inmates can't read*. It
doesn't take much imagination to anticipate what the future
is for a person who can't read. Where are the prophets who
can, by anticipating negative outcomes for illiterate children,
prevent them from becoming criminals by simply teaching
them to read? Perhaps if we had more tutors we would need
fewer prison guards.

4. ***Develop a keen sense of observation.*** My father would drive
my mother crazy with this little game. She would go out and
get her hair done, and when she returned he would look up
and ask, "When are you going to get your hair done?" If I saw
him do it once I saw him do it a hundred times.

It was a standing joke in the family.

What's not so funny is the number of people who really
don't see the other person in the relationship—not in a way
that matters. Paul Reiser had a situation on his sitcom "Mad
About You" where a series of questions revealed that he could
not even describe what his wife did for a living, much less
what she wore that day.

A prophet must learn to observe not merely the obvious,
but also the not so obvious.

The best example of this type training came from a coach
in a little town in Kentucky. This basketball team was so pitiful
that they hadn't won a game in years. Finally, a new coach
moved into town. Coach Story told the boys, "When you walk
home from practice today, I want you to pick up a couple of
stones and throw them at the fence post behind you. Don't
turn your head or look at the post, though. See if you can hit

it." Several parents scratched their head over the value of this exercise, but the coach was only developing the students' peripheral vision. Soon the team's "behind the back" passes became legendary. They ultimately won the state championship that year.

As a parent and a prophet, how good is your peripheral vision? Can you see what's happening around and behind you, or do you look only at the fence posts clearly in sight?

It is too often in hindsight that we realize prophetic clues that were there all along, had we only seen them. Mihaly Csikszentmihalyi, author of *Flow*, recalls leaving Hungary in the fall of 1944, when he was only ten years old. He said that scores of his well-educated and well-placed relatives came to the train station to say goodbye, and kept asking his family, "Why are you going to Venice in September? The theater season is already over and there are mosquitoes this time of year! You should stay here!" Mihaly recalls that all around Russian troops were circling the city. Right after the train pulled out, the bridge exploded, making Mihaly's train the last one to leave Budapest. Within months, all of the relatives concerned about operas and mosquito seasons were dead. This group of well-educated people had failed to observe the prophetic clues which Mihaly's family took seriously and acted upon.

Keen powers of observation turned a railroad engineer into a positive prophet for an elderly woman. In a story recounted in *Guidepost* 2-98, Dale Pape was rolling along a route he had worked for six years when something caught his eye. He said, "The driveway of a trailer home near the tracks hadn't been cleared of snow. That bothered me. During the summer months I had noticed that the yard had always been mowed." His logical mind told him that perhaps the owner had gone to Florida for the winter, which many people in the area did. Still something didn't seem right. A thought told him he should stop and investigate. However, stopping a train takes valuable time and fuel. Besides, his wife was waiting for him in town to attend an important event. He also needed to be the first to cross the "diamond" intersection, or he might have to wait, sometimes as long as three hours. However, the thought became more persistent: "GO BACK!" Finally, Dale pulled up on the brake amid much clanking and thundering and hissing, and backed the train down the track. Leaving the train to trudge through the snow, he found a 78-year-old woman who had gone out to shovel her walk, and fallen.

She had been lying in the snow for three hours. Paramedics said she would only have lasted fifteen more minutes. The woman said, "All I could do was pray that somebody would come along." Dale's powers of observation, combined with her prayer, turned into a lifesaving decision.

International negotiator Julian Gresser presented a thesis regarding the necessary powers of observation at the Intuition Network conference. He believes that Americans are so obsessed with winning that they can't stay in the moment and see what's happening around them. Preoccupied, they miss subtle clues to their opponents' intentions, and often lose the whole case as a result. Keen observation is a hallmark of prophesying a successful future.

5. *Exercise your physical being.* No one could accuse the proph-

ets in the Old Testament, or New, of being frail and sickly. A mere review of their journeys and activities reveals all of them to be hearty individuals who were often outdoors. The prophet Daniel was among four young Israelites captured and taken to the court of Nebuchadnezzer for training. The steward's job was to fatten up the young men so they would look hale and hearty for "Nebuchadnezzer University." Daniel, however, refused to eat the king's delicacies or drink the king's wine. When the steward protested that if Daniel and his friends didn't look healthy, he could lose his head (not to mention his job), Daniel asked him to provide them with water and vegetables only for a ten day period, and then compare their health to those of the other college preparatory students.

"Now at the end of ten days their features appeared better than all the young men who ate the portion of the king's delicacies. As for these four young men, God gave them knowledge and skill in all literature and wisdom; and Daniel had understanding in all visions and dreams." *(Daniel 1: 15–17)*

According to a study conducted by Joan Gondola, Ph.D., of Baruch College in New York, students taking aerobic fitness and dance classes were able to come up with more uses for an ordinary, everyday object, such as a pencil, than those who didn't work out regularly. Some experts think that the increased flow of oxygen to the brain is responsible, since an aerobically trained body transports and uses oxygen more efficiently than the body of somone whose heart rate rarely increases from exercise. Scientists have also found that when increased oxygen reaches the brain it has a beneficial effect on mood and recall.

6. *Imagine new possibilities.* The entry in Webster's College

Dictionary for "imagine" says "to form a mental image of something not yet actually present to the senses."

Canadian environmental expert Daniel Cappon has developed an IQ2 test to measure intuitive ability. In the test, Cappon helps identify ten input skills and output skills that people have. In a test for hindsight, a picture is presented of a devastated valley below a hill. Students are asked to imagine which caused the devastation: logging, forest fire, tree disease, volcano, or chemicals. The next two pictures show more and more clues, and the last one shows the volcano erupting. The person who knew the volcano was the cause from the very first picture would score higher, obviously, than the ones who required more clues. The high scorers on this test were the ones who had been able to imagine what had caused the devastation without having all the clues.

Walt Kallistead, senior pastor of The Community Church of Joy in Glendale, Arizona, has envisioned and helped create one of the largest and most exciting churches in the United States. Walt has envisioned a 300-acre community that includes everything from pre-school care to an elderly retirement center, in the midst of which is an entertainment center, an Olympic sports complex, an international leadership training center, and a town which is run entirely by the youth. The mayor of Glendale recently presented Walt with a plaque which read "To the man who always asks the question, 'What would it be like if . . . ?' "

Albert Einstein once said, "Imagination is everything." When asked if he would donate his brain to science after he died, Einstein agreed, warning people that they would find nothing extraordinary in its shape and size. In fact, his brain was slightly smaller than the average male's. Yet what could not be weighed or measured was his imagination.

Look at a person and imagine what a positive future for them might look like. Chances are you will catch a glimpse of something that is already there. William Wordsworth wrote "Trailing clouds of glory do we come." Perhaps prophecy is the ability to see the glory still there, hovering around us.

7. *Expand your interests and circle of friends.* Alan Vaugh, author of *Incredible Coincidence: The Baffling World of Synchronicity*, states that just having an active interest in something seems to make synchronicities happen more often—in part, because we notice them more. He also states that letting new people into your life increases your chances of having "synchronicities" occur, because the more people you know, the more they can help you "by chance." Many of the great inventors and artists and statesmen who helped create "reality" as we know it had a voracious curiosity and interest in disciplines beyond their main area of expertise. They were not "one trick ponies."

Benjamin Franklin not only prophesied the birth of a great nation, he also invented the United States postal system, the banking system, helped discover electricity, invented the first bifocals, and connected the rocking chair to a butter churner so farmers' wives could relax and make butter at the same time. Franklin spoke fluent French, and was amiable enough that he was considered one of our greatest ambassadors, cultivating an alliance with the French which ultimately proved critical for the success of the struggling American revolutionary army. Leonardo da Vinci not only painted and sculpted—he also prophesied and designed one of the first flying machines.

I get concerned when young people are urged to "special-
ize" at such an early age that they miss the wider world, and
the wisdom it can offer. I believe we all can, and should be,
renaissance people—capable of artistry and mastery in multiple fields of endeavor. Melinda Gates, wife of billionaire Bill
Gates, evidently feels the same way. She has established $20
million dollars worth of scholarships to help students explore
multiple fields, rather than specializing in just one. One professor with whom I was visiting shook his head and said, "So
often today the students say, 'I'm going to get the literature
and arts courses out of the way so then I can focus on my
major.' 'What's the rush?' I ask them." He sighed and looked
out the window as he said this. "What a waste of human potential . . ."

A speaker at a seminar I recently attended stated that the
great leaders of early America had two things in common. One
was that they all came from farming backgrounds. The other
was that they were each avid students of literature and the
classics. In fact, he said that the American aristocracy—those
born to wealth and status—often encourage their children to
have broad educations. In doing so they contribute to their
leadership skills and mentality, which perpetuates contributions to society.

8. **_Trust your intuition._** According to an article called "Intuition
at Work" by Frantz & Pattakos, studies done in the business
world show that when MBA students and experienced CEOs
are asked to solve a problem, both groups typically arrive at
the same answer. However, the CEOs solve the problem in a
much shorter time. Their intuition, based on experience, helps
them predict outcomes much more quickly than those who

have to study the facts. The older we get, the more our understanding of patterns and outcomes increases. Don't waste this valuable library of knowledge. Sometimes intuition is based solely on experience.

When you know something to be true, don't doubt it. Studies have shown that people who change their first answers to a quiz, frowning and doubting their first impressions, were usually right the first time. I once felt led to have a woman I was counseling throw Kleenex boxes against the wall. The inner directive to do this was clear. Later I learned that the woman's mother had abandoned her in a hospital when, as a five year old, she had thrown Kleenex boxes against the wall. Apparently, the adult woman needed a cathartic event in a safe place to assist in her healing. There was no way I could have known this with my natural mind. I just trusted my intuition, and it turned out to be right.

As I say in my book *Grow Something Besides Old*, intuition is wisdom in retrospect.

9. **Drift.** According to author Philip Goldberg, successful business leaders rely a great deal on what is called "soft data": rumors, gossip, facial expressions and trends that have nothing to do with the business at hand. He also noted that those with the greatest success tended to be neutral and attentive, often allowing a sense of meaning to unfold. Author Rudyard Kipling got some of his most inspired ideas when he allowed himself to "drift." John O'Donohue shares in his beautiful book *Anam Cara*, that the wonderful conductor Sergiu Celibadache said, "We do not create music; we only create the conditions so that she can appear." By stilling our mind, we can more clearly sense God's.

We do not always have to be rowing in order to get where we're going. Sometimes the wind can carry us, sometimes the stream. Nor do we always have to answer when somebody calls.

I recently was amused to read an ad in the lost and found section of our local newspaper. It read "Lost. White cockatiel bird. Female. Tame. May respond to 'Come here.' "

"And then again," I thought, "maybe she won't." Maybe she will fly away to some larger, distant tree. Maybe she is enjoying the view with no bars confining her. We are all too tame, perhaps, allowing the vertical lines in our appointment books to dictate how we see the world. Maybe that's what Jesus was saying when He saw us toiling away and said with a hint of laughter in His voice, and an echo of great joy to come, "Drop your nets and follow me. Let's drift for awhile and find God's will."

10. **Be persistent.** Recently on NPR I heard the story about a snail who was making its way up the steps to the king's palace. The young king saw the snail, picked it up, and angrily hurled it out to the sea. Seven years later the snail returns, crawls up to the astonished king, and asks, "What was that all about?"

Do not let circumstances interfere with your vision of the future. *USA Today* reported a story about eleven people who were attending a wedding in Harvey Cedars, New Jersey. At one point, the second floor deck above the ceremony suddenly collapsed. The entire wedding party was sent to the hospital, many of them with broken arms, legs, neck and back injuries. This did not stop the nuptials from occuring, however, as the bride and groom exchanged vows in the emergency room at the county hospital. The policeman, who also served as a witness, said, "Everybody was already there, so they decided to go ahead with the wedding."

Alexander Graham Bell, the inventor of the telephone, said that "illumination comes when you are in a state of mind in which you know exactly what you want, and are fully determined not to quit until you get it."

11. **Prepare**. Craig Maginnis recently noted in *Reader's Digest*, "The coach of our public high school's junior varsity basketball team arranged for us to play a preseason game against his alma mater, the local Catholic high school. Early in the game we noticed the captain of the other team make the sign of the cross before shooting a free throw. 'Hey, coach,' one of my teammates on the bench asked, 'what does that mean?' His quick reply: 'Not a darn thing if he can't shoot.' "

Peekaboo Street had long imagined the triumph of winning a gold medal in the Olympics. Her vision was intense. However, shortly before the Olympics she injured her knee in a bad fall. Unable to ski the actual practice runs herself, she persuaded her coach to ski down the slope with her on his back, so that she could be better prepared for the final race. She won, of course, but not without adding preparation to her prophecy.

I am amazed, sometimes, at the lack of preparedness we each display. Despite the Indian saying "It is a good day to die," some 70 percent of people still die without a will. Every year hundreds die in fires that could have been prevented if only someone had installed a fire alarm, or kept the batteries current.

Not too long ago I was asked to conduct a leadership retreat for fifty hand-selected leaders from a major hospital
chain. This was to be a three-day workshop, yet twenty-five
of the people actually came without even bringing a pen, a
pencil, paper, or anything to write on! I looked out over the
surprised faces who were scrambling about for a pen and
thought, "These are supposed to be leaders?" Can you imagine a fire chief who at the last minute had to look for a map—
or couldn't find his boots when the alarm went off?

Jesus consistently told us to live in a state of preparedness.
I have an eclectic missionary friend who sleeps with his boots
on. "When the rapture comes I don't want to go to heaven
barefooted. Who knows what we'll have to tramp through
on the way there!" I laughed at his thought. But that night,
I put my boots out by the bed. "A prophet must be prepared," I thought, as I also laid out some numbers to call if
people one day couldn't find me. "Two men will be working together in the fields, and one will be taken, the other
left. Two women will be going about their household tasks;
one will be taken, the other left. So be prepared, for you
don't know what day your Lord is coming." *(Matthew
24:40–41)*

12. ***Pray.*** I was recently startled to learn that despite what it
looks like to the human eye, lightning does not so much flash
down from heaven as it flashes upward from earth. According to lightning authority Jeff Renecke, "The flash of light
which is ultimately three to four miles long and carries more
than 100 million volts of electricity is a response to a buildup
of negatively charged, hovering clouds. The tension between

the negative ionization of the clouds above and the positive charges in the earth below creates the combination of upward streamers and downward flashes which we see as a flash of lightning. Lightning is *escaping from* and striking the earth more than 8.6 million times a day." In other words, lightning goes up as well as down.

In the best-selling book *Embraced by the Light*, author Betty Eadies claims that when she "died" and visited heaven she saw many individual streams of light coming up from the earth. She was told by her heavenly guides that these streams of light represented the prayers of each person on the planet.

Psychiatrist Elisabeth Targ of California Pacific Medical Center in San Francisco recently reported that AIDS patients who were prayed for were healthier a few months later than equally ill patients who had received no prayers. "Our understanding of consciousness is incomplete," she writes. "There may be more contact between people (who are praying) than we might ordinarily assume."

In Revelations 8: 3–4 we are told, "Another angel, who had a golden censer, came and stood at the altar. From the angel's hand the smoke of the incense went up in the presence of God, and with it the prayers of the saints."

"I was still at prayer, when Gabriel, the being I had originally seen in a vision, swooped on me in full flight at the hour of the evening sacrifice." *(Daniel 9:20–21)*

Daniel's vision became real while he was still praying.

At the Community Church of Joy, Arlene Skaff, the prayer coordinator, got the idea of "Prayer Walkers." Every day at nine in the morning people show up and are assigned to walk with a prayer partner. While they walk they are encouraged to pray out loud for anything or anyone that crosses their minds. Previously, prayer walkers had gathered in a room, and prayed aloud from a prepared script. Arlene and her new team found a more exciting way to make prayer come alive—with exercise. "You would not believe the results we are getting!" she exclaimed. Oh, yes I would. Prayer often becomes prophecy.

"I tell you therefore, everything you ask and pray for, believe that you have it already, and it will be yours." *(Mark 11:24)*

Prayer is prophecy.

A Personal Prophecy Readiness Quiz:

Rate yourself in the following categories on a scale of one to ten, with one being low and ten being high.

1. *Keep good company.*
Who do you spend most of your time around? What are their major goals and concerns? What does your conversation with them center around? What kind of prophecies do they give you, and one another? With what results?

_____

_____

I rate myself a _____ (1–10) in this category, because: _____

_____

In order to improve my score, I see myself: _____

_____

2. *Seek wisdom.*

What wisdom literature do you study? How often? Do you read the Bible weekly, or "weakly"? How many words of wisdom can you recite by memory?

_____

_____

I rate myself a _____ (1–10) in this category, because:_____

_____

In order to improve my score, I see myself: _____

3. *Anticipate outcomes.*

How often do you look at a scenario and anticipate its outcome? Do you just look at the present facts of a matter, or do you look down the road and imagine various end results? Are you a short-range or a long-range thinker?

_____

_____

I rate myself a _____ (1–10) in this category, because: _____

_____

In order to improve my score, I see myself: _____

4. *Develop a keen sense of observation.*

A policeman can look at a city scene and make keen observations about the people in it, traffic flow, any suspicious characters lurking in the shadows, any open doors or unlocked windows that might invite a burglar, etc. An artist might look at the same scene and see the way the light is hitting the leaves on the trees, notice the patterns the shadows are making, and see if there are any color patterns in the clothes of the people walking down the sidewalk. When you walk through a scene, what are you observing? Or are you, like too many of us, lost in your own thoughts about what else you should be doing?

_____

_____

I rate myself a _____ (1–10) in this category, because: _____

_____

In order to improve my score, I see myself: _____

5. *Exercise your physical being.* If a prophet looked at your current food and exercise schedule of the last five days, what would he or she anticipate your health to be five years from now? Ten years from now? Twenty years from now? How much exercise are you getting on a daily basis? Are you clogging your arteries and starving your cells for oxygen, and wondering why your performance at work or home is suffering?

_____

_____

I rate myself a _____ (1–10) in this category, because: _____

_____

In order to improve my score, I see myself: _____

6. *Imagine new possibilities.* How do you exercise your imagination? Do you, or do you depend on others to do it for you? When was the last time you imagined a new possibility for yourself—or others? Can you look at a rubber band and come up with seventeen possible uses? Could you do the same with a paper clip?

_____

_____

I rate myself a _____ (1–10) in this category, because: _____
_____

In order to improve my score, I see myself: _____

7. *Expand your interests and circle of friends.*
Who have you met lately that was new and interesting? How
many new people do you meet and converse with in a month?
If you were going to have a dinner party and invite Barbara Wal-
ters, who among your close friends would you invite, and what
would she be able to interview them about? What would she be
able to interview you about? What new activity is really exciting
you these days? What are you learning that is new?

_____

_____

I rate myself a _____ (1–10) in this category, because: _____
_____

In order to improve my score, I see myself: _____

8. *Trust your intuition.* How much do you trust yourself to make
decisions on a daily basis? What do your friends ask your advice
about? How often do you hear—and obey—simple inner direc-
tives?

_____

_____

I rate myself a _____ (1–10) in this category, because: _____
_____

In order to improve my score, I see myself: _____

9. *Drift.*
How much unprogrammed time is in your day? When was the last

time you lay out in the sun and just thought of nothing? When do you let your mind relax, and how? How might you learn to program in nonprogrammed time, and why is it important that you do?

_____

_____

I rate myself a _____ (1–10) in this category, because: _____

_____

In order to improve my score, I see myself: _____

10. *Be persistent.*

How many times did Moses go back to Pharaoh before he actually let the people go? Would people say persistence is one of your greater qualities? If so, what examples of that would come to mind?

_____

_____

I rate myself a _____ (1–10) in this category, because: _____

_____

In order to improve my score, I see myself: _____

11. *Prepare.*

How prepared are you to excel in the area which most holds your interest? How much study do you do on a weekly or monthly basis? Are you prepared for the One who comes asking questions?

_____

_____

I rate myself a _____ (1–10) in this category, because: _____

_____

In order to improve my score, I see myself: _____

12. *Pray.*

If an outsider were to measure your prayer life, how many minutes or hours a day would they find you solely absorbed in the activity? If God were measuring your prayer life on a Richter scale, would you even rate a tremor? Do you believe that your prayer counts for anything? If so, how much?

_____

_____

I rate myself a _____ (1–10) in this category, because:_____

_____

In order to improve my score, I see myself: _____

Scoring and Evaluating Your Results

Total up your points for the twelve categories. Write the total points here: _____

90–120 Points: You sound and think like a prophet. Congratulations! Get busy doing what you know how to do!

75–90 Points: You are on your way. Turn up your efforts three notches, and watch the results in your life and in others' lives blossom.

60–75 Points: Come on—get confident. You can do better than this. You are holding yourself back. What are you afraid of?

45–60 Points: You are lukewarm in your efforts here, and probably elsewhere in your life. Turn your engines on. Life is meant to be an adventure!

30–45 Points: Pick one area to really excel at. Watch your other scores go up in the other categories, as well.

0–30 Points: Are you being too hard on yourself? If not, wake up. The world awaits you!

Go out! Go out!
Prepare the roadway for my people
to return.
Build the roads,
pull out the boulders,
lift up a standard for
the people.
—*Isaiah 62:10*

Words of Caution:
How Not to Misuse the Gift

Jesus warned against false prophets—those who lead people astray with predictions and prophecies which are based not on the word or the will of God but are merely designed to benefit the "fortune" teller.

In our times we have had too many examples of false prophets. Adolf Hitler claimed to prophesy a better life for "good Germans," and they believed him, engaging in unbelievable acts of violence, rape, torture, and murder to help bring his false prophecies about.

Who among us hasn't been stung by some business deal which was absolutely certain to make us rich quick? There is a proverb which reads, "It is difficult for a salesman not to incur sin." Remember, salespeople are prophesying some future benefit to you when they talk. Make sure their words are real.

In the spiritual realm it really gets sticky. I remember attending meetings where prophecies were called out over couples by traveling preachers who, oddly enough, often prophesied that the couples were meant to come help them build their church. The New Age movement boasted a guru who channeled an entity who often advised followers to invest in her horse farm in the Northwest. Jimmy Bakker sold more time shares than he had time (or space for) in his and Tammy Faye's Promised Land. Corrupt popes in the middle ages got rich by selling indulgences, or "short cuts" to heaven to the willing wealthy. I've met a number of self-proclaimed holy men of God about which I can only say, "They love God—it's people they can't stand." Sometimes people have "prophesied" that God wanted me to write a book with them, or better yet, marry them. (Usually, this has not been confirmed in my heart, as it were.)

Even holy people let their weaknesses slip through. Every message received by even the holiest of spokespeople must be screened and filtered. One of the writer's most important tools is the wastebasket. What is not true must be discarded.

Bonus Tips: How to Know When You're Receiving a Prophecy

How to know if you're receiving a word from the Lord

Internal Symptoms

The following symptoms may apply when you are delivering, or receiving a prophecy.

You may experience:	*Case in Point:*
Terror	Daniel (Daniel 4:5 8:17), The Disciples (Mat 4:41)
Disbelief	Zacharias (Luke 1:18)
A quickening of the heart	Mary (Luke 1:29)
Tingling in the lips	Isaiah 6:5–6
Dry mouth	Moses (Exodus 4:10)
Feeling faint or weak in the knees	Daniel 6:23, Nehemiah 2:3
A sense of extreme calm and inner knowing	Mary (Luke 1:46)
A sense of ecstasy	Simeon (Luke 2:28), Saul (1 Samuel 10:5–6)
A sense of wonder	Shepherds (Luke 2:8–15)
A sense of delight	Elizabeth (Luke 1:4)
A sense of being transported to another place	Elijah (2 Kings 2:11), Ezekiel 40:2

A sudden insight	Peter (Mark 8:29)
A gradual realization	Followers of Jesus (Luke 24:1–30)

As a prophet, you may:

See your words come true	Joshua 4:10–18, Joshua 11:23, Noah (Gen 7:5–12), Isaiah (Mat 7:6)
Not see your words come true	Jonah (Jonah 4:1), Pilate's wife (Mat 27–10)
Be celebrated and revered	Samuel (1 Sam 3:19), Jonathan (2 Sam 1:26), Mary (Luke 1:48)
Be ridiculed and murdered	Jesus (John 19:1–42)

Once you are a prophet, you must:

Say what you are given to say	Moses (Exodus 4:10)
Follow explicitly the directions you receive	Noah (Genesis 6:22)
Trust	Elijah (1 Kings 18:22–36)
Act always in love	John (1 John 4:7–8), Paul (1 Corinthians 13:2)

You are most likely to receive a prophecy when you are: about to go to sleep, about to wake up, praying, gardening, jogging, resting, taking a shower, dancing, singing, working, reading, alone, in a group, playing with children, walking in a field, and engaging in any activity where you are open to God.

God yearns for us to prophesy and encourage one another. Yet, where are the prophets among us? There were none for the little girl in the story that follows.

A Prophecy Unfulfilled: What Happens When There Is No Prophet?

"Where then is my hope?"
Job 17:15

$\mathcal{N}$ot too long ago in my hometown, a perfect newborn baby girl was left alone on the banks of a river to breathe her last. Found unexpectedly by two men who were out quail hunting, the little bundle was scooped up quickly by the hunters and raced to the hospital. I picture them having to rearrange their coolers and ammunition to make way for this child wrapped in cloth. The hospital officials only confirmed what the hunters already knew. The little girl—later named Monica Angelique—was dead.

This story made the front page of the "Living" Section in the newspaper. Many people were interviewed to try to determine who the mother was—and where. Was she trembling alone in some project apartment? Had she thumbed a ride from some unknowing trucker and now was putting the asphalt road between her and a bad memory?

The news cameras came out to cover the story when they heard the hunters were going back to the river to build the baby a cross. The reporters fell strangely silent as the only sound being broadcast was the sound of the cross being hammered into the dirt. The man who had done the hammering walked silently with his head down toward his little two-year-old girl. He lifted her up to the sky, and then dropped her down back into his arms and showered her with kisses, his body racked by sobs as he walked away.

It has been four months since the story ran and the mother is still unknown. The hundreds of people who came forward to announce that they would have gladly taken little Monica in will never know that baby's touch, nor will she know theirs.

Who might this child have become, if only there had been a manger prepared for her? Or even a tiny boat made of reeds like the one made by another desperate mother, the mother of Moses, who had also gone down to the river to give her child away.

If only this young unknown mother had understood there was a safety net of support. Perhaps she was a child herself, who had ultimately walked away because no one had ever given her a positive prophecy.

The baby girl found dead by the river had been born on Thanksgiving Day.

Little Monica Angelique became a prophecy unfulfilled because no positive prophecy was ever spoken for her or her mother—at least not in a way that had been understood and received.

Final Thoughts: A Summary of How Prophecy Affects Us

My mother used to bring home clothes for my sister and brother and me. A fashion designer by profession (before the Depression forced her to go into bookkeeping), she loved to put together outfits for us, and imagine how we would look in them. It was not unusual for us kids to come home and find three or four outfits on our bed. We would try on all of them, and decide which ones we would keep and wear.

I think about the verse in Psalm 139: "O Lord, you laid out all my days for me, when as yet there were none of them." God certainly has wonderful visions in mind for us, which are laid out like outfits on our bed. Ultimately, however, *we* choose what we will wear. God, no matter how imaginative He is, will not make choices for us.

On my desk sits a little frog, dressed in an angel costume. She has a gold wire halo around her head, and is holding a wooden scepter wrapped loosely around her hand with gold ribbon. Silver stars are spilled in profusion all over her white crinoline skirt. Her big blue eyes are slightly crossed as she sits here looking up at me with a green-lipped grin.

That frog reminds me of me, a prophet in disguise. That frog reminds me of us, able to help bring about the dreams of others while we still contemplate our own "frogness."

All that is needed, all that is necessary, is that we wake up and recognize that it is, indeed, morning in our throats. And then we can begin to prophesy all over God's good green earth.

The Prophetic Pledge

"Neglect not the gift that is in thee, that was
given thee by prophecy."

1 Timothy 4:14

Prophecy Remembrance Sheets

These are the following prophecies and positive comments given to me by others:

These are the prophecies I choose to believe:

My Prophetic Pledge

I pledge to give out at least three positive prophecies a day.

I pledge to look at people the way God sees them, and to communicate that vision to them in loving and sincere ways.

I pledge to consider myself a prophet in all I say and do.

_____   _____
Name   Date

_____
Witness

Acknowledgments

*I*n the frenetic and often harried business of publishing it is easy to overlook the prophetic abilities of the agents who see and promote the writer's vision, the editors who so patiently help shape it, and the publishers who put their money behind it. I believe that at the heart of the publishing business is a desire to be messengers for good—as well as profit. This work would not have come to being if it were not for the prescience of Julie Castiglia, who helped originally sell the idea to Hyperion, to Mary Ann Naples, who also acted as champion, coach, and taskmaster, to David Cashion, my editor, who risked life and limb by sending me memos asking for "more . . ." and of course Bob Miller, who has stood behind my work unfailingly and with great faithfulness. To them I offer my great and grateful appreciation.

To Dee Jones, my personal prophet and administrator who continues to see the vision for the future and hold it amidst all the chaos that I can generate, and to Kathryn Antonacci, our faithful director of communications and promoter of seminars and sender of materials, thank you.

To my original Rainbow friends who helped support me in Dallas as I wrote songs and hoped for a miracle twenty-five years ago, I offer a special prayer of gratitude. Linda Sterrett Marple, Beau Black, Larry Gene, Edwin, Sharon, Sandra Marlene Harrison . . . thank you for being prophets with me.

To my El Paso family: Kathy, Ben, Bennie, Wade, Tara Ivey, Joe Jones, and Margara; Irma Soto, Irene, Jacob, Ricardo, and Joseph Prat; Manuelita, Yvonne, Miguel, Gabriela, and Antonio Gomez. You all bring me such inexpressible joy. Thank you for your constant support and belief. It takes a village to support a writer, and you do that for me in ways that give me a rootedness that is satisfying to the bone. P.S. Thanks for always making sure I get to the airport on time.

To Willy Bonkers and Colene Absolam, who sat and waited with me in the desert, thank you. To Betty Ann Bird and Lisa Dahlberg, who pulled me through a narrow hole in the honey tree, thank you.

To Susanna Palomares and Dave Cowan, Ken and Margie Blanchard, Bill Pollard, Dominic Giambona, Ron Mannix, Deborah Bartlett, Bill Campbell, Doug Hawthorne, Mike Regan, Russ and Laura Chaisson, Mike Mann and Rick Prescott, Ed Blitz, Joe Mairano, Jeff Cohen, Barbara Reynolds, Steve Shull, Hugh Daniels, Edgar Songe, Randy Altig, Marilyn Beaubien, Candi Staton Susswel, Arnold Goldstein, and all the other beings who make my world such an exciting and beautiful place, thank you. I also owe a special debt of gratitude to Dr. Norman Vincent Peale, Ruth Stafford Peale, and Ron Glasser of *Guideposts* for their continuous inspiration.

To our Path facilitators: Cindi Acree-Hamann, James Ami, Hal Anderson, Barbara-Lynn Anderson, Kathleen Archibald Simon, Mercedes Arroyo, Mike Aufderhar, Marianne Auten, Wayne Belcher, Verdale Benjamin, Irene Bertolucci, Sandra Block, Laurie Boddie, Valorie Boucher, Starita Boyce, Julie Boyden, Kevin Bradley, Judy Bragg, Jackie Brewton, Jim Bruggenschmidt, Pearl Bryant, Joan Bryden, Hannah Buchanan, Andrew

Bullians, Elaine Burau, Thomas Cerny, Greg Cheney, Linda Ciabatoni, Regenia Clark, Claudia Coe, Jeff Cohen, Adrienne Colby, Melissa Collins, Susan Corning, Roger L. Davis, Carol Davis, Darlene Davis, Dick Dawson, Bonnie Dawson, Shawn Dove, Lu Dunbar, Marianne Dunn, Jackie Elfatouri, Jim Ellick, Terri Elton, Leslie Enzbrenner, Kerry Faudree, Dennis Feaster, Sheila Fleishman, Lyn Fordham, Nina Frost, Tim Garrison, Shani Garza, Sheila Gerald, Marianne Glick, Billy Godwin, Lori Goertzen, Sandra Gooding, Carol Graser, Charley Green, M. J. Griffin, La Verne Gryte, Sheri Gryte, Davender Gupta, Francy Hall, Debra Harless, David Harris, Georgia Harris, Sally Hazard Bourgoin, Tom Heck, Julie Helps, John Hersey, Merilyn Hill, Beverly Hobbs Shea, Carol Hoefer, JR Holt, Larry Holycross, Dennis and Brenda Houk, Tom Howell, Joyce Hulse, Parker Hurlburt, Susan Ickes, Barbara Inglis, Narciso Inlong, Bill Izard, Sarah James, Sandy Jasmer, Robert Jewell, Caesar Kalinowski, Kate Katz, Janie Kauffman Carver, Charlene Keto, Patti Kindelberger, Norma Kirbs, Jill Kohlberger, Pamela Laubscher, Rebecca Lawrence, Ingrid Linhart, David Loughery, Carole Maggio, Betty Mahalik, Gerardo Maldonado, Frank Mallinder, Mike Mann, Stephanie Maras, Kathy Marcil, Ouida McClendon, David McClure, Jacquie McCord, Sean McCosh, Janet McEwen, Jonathan McGraw, Betty McKean, Elizabeth McLeod, Barbara McRae, Corinth Milikin, David Mills, Donnis Minx, Lisa Morgan, Abraham Moyano, Petra Norman, Robert Odum, Paula Ohlmeyer, Tom Osborn, Pamela Paduano Savage, Karmen Palumbo, Susan Pedaline, Marilyn Powers, Irene Prat, Rick Prescott, Nancy Purcell, Gerald Redman, Tom Reid, Toni Richerson, Christian Richter, Roberto Rivera, Abraham Romo, Lorraine Rothenberg, Rosemarie Rowley, Bonnie Sachs, Kristi Saunders, Joshua Sayegusa, Patty Schlesser, Larry and Paula Schneider, Tara Seon, Pat Shadle, Phyllis Shippy, Steve Shull, Scott Singletary, Kaylene Smith, Gloria Smith, Mima Soto, Joleen Spencer, Debra Squires, Ann Starrette, Lee Sterling, Debbie Stevens, Paula Stevenson, Maureen Sullivan, Donna Summers, Elizabeth Ann Summers, Howard Sutter, Kim Tinkham, Ro Trent Vaselaar, Sarah Underwood, Diane Urban, Idelette Van Papendorp, Charles Waldo, Marjorie Wall Hofer, Pat Westfall, Pat Whelan, Felecia White, Gerry Wienholt, Lacinda Wilson, Tessa Wingate, Kenny Wong, Ann Wong, Marjorie Woo, Sarah Wood, Gail Worth, and Bonnie Worthley. Thank you very much for all of your hard work and support.

To Catherine Calhoun, who has been a prophet to me nearly all my life, thank you.

But most of all, I owe my being and seeing to my mother, Irene Jones. I am rich with prophecy because of her love.

Gift Offer

For more information, to get on our mailing list, or to order any of the following please contact:

The Jesus, CEO Foundation

813 Summersong Court

Encinitas, CA 92024

Phone: 760-753-7251

Fax: 760-634-2707

e-mail dee@lauriebethjones.com

website www.lauriebethjones.com

If you would like to receive a free bookmark from *The Power of Positive Prophecy*, please send us a stamped, self-addressed #10 (11-inch-long) envelope, and we will also include you on our mailing list.

We also have the following products and services available:

Keynote speaking

Full- or half-day on-site leadership training programs

Study guides for *Jesus, CEO* and *The Path* (also available in Spanish)

Facilitator's training in *Jesus, CEO* and *The Path*

On-line college courses on *Jesus, CEO* and *The Path*

Personal telephone consultations with Laurie

A master's/mentor program for individuals

Song tape and coloring book for children

A newsletter

"I was neither a
prophet, nor a
prophet's son.
I was a shepherd, and I
also took care of sycamore trees.
But the Lord took me from
tending the flock and
said to me 'Go, prophesy.' "

Amos 7:14–15

Index